The future of
higher education

Presented to Parliament by
the Secretary of State for Education and Skills
by Command of Her Majesty
January 2003

Cm 5735

£17.50

Contents

Foreword by the Secretary of State for Education and Skills

British universities are a great success story. Over the last 30 years some of the finest brains in the world have pushed the boundaries of knowledge, science and understanding. At the same time a university place has ceased to be the preserve of a tiny elite but been extended to hundreds of thousands more students each year. In the early 1960s only 6 per cent of under-21s went to university, whereas today around 43 per cent of 18–30 year olds in England enter higher education.

So it would be possible to opt for a quiet life. To coast along, bask in previous successes, shirk the need for reform. Though such an approach would be possible, I do believe that it would be wrong.

It would be wrong because the world is already changing faster than it has ever done before, and the pace of change will continue to accelerate.

Our national ability to master that process of change and not be ground down by it depends critically upon our universities. Our future success depends upon mobilizing even more effectively the imagination, creativity, skills and talents of all our people. And it depends on using that knowledge and understanding to build economic strength and social harmony.

So that immediately identifies two areas where our universities have to improve.

First, the expansion of higher education has not yet extended to the talented and best from all backgrounds. In Britain today too many of those born into less advantaged families still see a university place as being beyond their reach, whatever their ability.

Second, we have to make better progress in harnessing knowledge to wealth creation. And that depends on giving universities the freedoms and resources to compete on the world stage. To back our world class researchers with financial stability. To help turn ideas into successful businesses. To undo the years of under-investment that will result in our universities slipping back.

But there is also a third challenge. To make the system for supporting students fairer. Having a university education brings big benefits and while the Government will continue to pay most of the cost involved in studying for a degree, it is also reasonable to ask students to contribute to this. But we need to make sure that no student is put off from going into higher education because they cannot afford the cost of studying while they are at university. And those who come from the poorest backgrounds should get extra support.

This White Paper declares our intention to take the tough decisions on higher education, to deal with student finance for the long term, to open up access to our universities, and to allow them to compete with the best. We seek a partnership between students, government, business and the universities to renew and expand our higher education system for the next generation.

I hope that the proposals which I set out here will help strengthen that partnership.

That is the foundation for our future national success.

Charles Clarke

Executive Summary

Higher education brings great benefits...

Our higher education system is a great asset, both for individuals and the nation. The skills, creativity, and research developed through higher education are a major factor in our success in creating jobs and in our prosperity. Universities and colleges play a vital role in expanding opportunity and promoting social justice. The benefits of higher education for individuals are far-reaching. On average, graduates get better jobs and earn more than those without higher education.

...and our universities are world renowned...

We can be proud of our universities. The number gaining degrees has tripled in the last two decades while safeguarding quality. Completion rates for students are among the best in the world. More overseas students are studying here. Our research capacity is strong and, at best, world class. Recent years have seen a dramatic increase in the number of new companies spun out of universities' innovation.

...but there is no room for complacency

The challenge from other countries is growing. Higher education is under pressure, and at risk of decline. We face hard choices on funding, quality and management:

- Higher education must expand to meet rising skill needs.

- The social class gap among those entering university remains too wide.

- Many of our economic competitors invest more in higher education.

- Universities are struggling to employ the best academics.

- Funding per student fell 36 per cent between 1989 and 1997.

- The investment backlog in teaching and research facilities is estimated at £8 billion.

- Universities need stronger links with business and economy.

Tackling these challenges needs a long-term strategy for investment and reform

The Government is reversing years of under-investment with an increase in funding for higher education averaging more than 6 per cent – over and above inflation – for the next three years. Funding for student support will rise sharply – including new grants for students from lower income families – and the science settlement is the most generous for a decade. This extra investment will boost access and enable universities to tackle many of their immediate problems.

But this alone will not enable universities to boost opportunity and excellence as much as we need. Additional resources will be needed if they are to meet the long-term challenge to maintain and improve high standards, expand and widen access, strengthen links with business, and compete globally.

There is no easy, painless way to put our universities and student finance system on a sustainable basis. If we duck the difficult decisions needed, the risk of decline will increase and students and the country at large will suffer.

The measures we put forward will:

■ Bring major improvements to the funding of research and knowledge transfer, boost world class excellence and strengthen the work of universities in supporting the regional economies;

■ Improve and reward excellent teaching;

■ Enable more people to enter higher education, benefiting both individuals and the economy's need for higher level skills;

■ Support those from disadvantaged backgrounds by restoring grants, helping with fee costs, and abolishing up-front tuition fees for all students. This will support our programme for increasing attainment and aspiration;

■ Allow universities to secure a contribution of between £0 and £3,000 per year to the cost of each course – paid fairly when graduates are in work linked to their ability to pay; and

■ Give universities long term financial certainty by helping them build up endowment funds.

Research Excellence – Building on our Strengths

British universities have huge strengths in research. New resources will help improve teaching and research at our universities but we also need to reap the benefits which flow from concentrating the best research in larger units – better infrastructure, better collaboration within and between disciplines, easier development of research-only posts and better pay for excellent researchers.

The Government will:

- Increase spending on research in 2005–06 by £1.25 billion compared to 2002–03 – around 30 per cent in real terms;

- Encourage and reward research in larger units, including through collaboration;

- Invest more in our leading research departments and universities, enabling them to compete with the world's best;

- Develop new incentives to support emerging and improving research;

- Develop and reward talented researchers, with rigorous new standards for government-funded research postgraduate places;

- Create a new Arts and Humanities Research Council.

Higher Education and Business – Exchanging and Developing Knowledge and Skills

Higher education in the UK generates over £34 billion for our economy and supports more than half a million jobs. But less than one in five businesses taps into universities' skills and knowledge. Universities and colleges can play a bigger role in creating jobs and prosperity.

We will encourage this by:

- Strengthening the Higher Education Innovation Fund (HEIF) – worth £90m a year in 2005–06 – to encourage especially the non research-intensive universities to work with employers locally, regionally and nationally;

- Funding through HEIF a network of 20 Knowledge Exchanges to reward and support HE institutions working with business;

- Building stronger partnerships between HE institutions and regional development agencies (RDAs), with RDAs playing an increasing role allocating HEIF;

- Helping sector skills councils forge stronger alliances between business and relevant departments in universities and colleges.

Teaching and learning – delivering excellence

Effective teaching and learning is essential if we are to promote excellence and opportunity in higher education. High quality teaching must be recognised and rewarded, and best practice shared.

Reforms include:

- Additional funding not just for excellence in research but also in teaching with new money for pay modernisation, rewarding good teaching and providing more fellowships for the best;

- Centres of Excellence to reward good teaching and promote best practice;

- Better information for students including a new annual student survey and publication of summaries of external examiners' reports to help student choice drive up quality;

- New national professional standards for teaching and a new national body to develop and promote good teaching – the Teaching Quality Academy.

Expanding higher education to meet our needs

The case for expanding higher education is strong. But we will not compromise on quality. We want the bulk of the expansion to come through new types of qualification, better tailored to the needs of students and the economy.

We will:

- Continue to increase participation towards 50 per cent of those aged 18–30, mainly through two-year work-focused foundation degrees;

- Work with employers to develop more foundation degrees, providing financial incentives for students, strengthening links between further and higher education and creating better pathways for progression;

- Encourage more flexibility in courses, to meet the needs of a more diverse student body and improve support for those doing part-time degrees.

Fair Access

The social class gap in entry to higher education remains unacceptably wide. While many more people from all backgrounds benefit from higher education, the proportion coming from lower-income families has not substantially increased. It means a waste of potential for individuals and for the country as a whole.

Raising participation and standards in our reforms of secondary and further education will be the most important step in improving access. Improvements to student finance will also remove barriers. But universities and colleges must do more if they are to play their full part in promoting opportunity.

Our package includes:

- Restoring grants for students from lower income families and abolishing up-front fees for all;

- Requiring universities to draw up an Access Agreement to improve access for disadvantaged students, before they are able to increase the level of fee they ask students to pay;

- Appointing an independent Access Regulator to oversee these agreements, to promote wider access and to ensure that admissions procedures are fair, professional and transparent;

- Expanding our national AimHigher programme to build better links between schools, colleges and universities and raise young people's aspirations;

- Reforming funding so that universities and colleges will be properly reimbursed for extra costs in attracting and retaining students from non-traditional backgrounds; and

- We have doubled the amount of extra money to help vulnerable students and will introduce a new package of grant support for part-time students.

Freedoms and Funding

The Government is tackling decades of under-investment and making an unprecedented investment in our universities. But universities require financial certainty for the long term as well as the short term. The Government will continue to be the major funder of universities but they should also have greater freedom to access new funding streams on their own account.

Providing incentives to build up endowments is one way. Another is allowing universities the right to secure from graduates larger contributions to the cost of their education. Graduates on average earn much more than those without degrees and are far more likely to be in employment. But we will not compromise on fair access and will take steps to ensure young people are not deterred by up-front fees.

We will:

- Re-introduce from 2004 a new grant of up to £1,000 a year for students from lower-income families, benefiting around a third of students;

- Introduce in 2006 a new Graduate Contribution Scheme. Universities will be allowed to seek a contribution of between £0 and £3,000 per year for each course;

- Continue to pay up to the first £1,100 of fees for students from lower income families;

- Abolish up-front payment of tuition fees and allow every student to defer until after they have graduated their contribution to the cost of their course. Payments after graduation will be through the tax system, linked to ability to pay;

- Raise, from April 2005, the threshold at which graduates have to start repaying their fee contribution and maintenance loan from £10,000 to £15,000;

- Help universities build up endowment funds by promoting individual and corporate giving and creating a fund to give universities the incentive to raise their own endowment finance.

Our ambition is to ensure that this country has a higher education system matching the best in the world. These proposals show how this ambition can be achieved.

Chapter 1
The need for reform

Values

1.1   Higher education is a great national asset. Its contribution to the economic and social well-being of the nation is of vital importance.

1.2   Its research pushes back the frontiers of human knowledge and is the foundation of human progress. Its teaching educates and skills the nation for a knowledge-dominated age. It gives graduates both personal and intellectual fulfilment. Working with business, it powers the economy, and its graduates are crucial to the public services. And wide access to higher education makes for a more enlightened and socially just society.

1.3   In a fast-changing and increasingly competitive world, the role of higher education in equipping the labour force with appropriate and relevant skills, in stimulating innovation and supporting productivity and in enriching the quality of life is central. The benefits of an excellent higher education system are far-reaching; the risk of decline is one that we cannot accept.

Our strengths

1.4   We are rightly proud of higher education in England. Our universities and colleges have been through a dramatic transformation over the last quarter-century as participation in higher education has tripled, and generally have maintained high quality and good value despite a halving of the unit of funding.

1.5   Universities also make a substantial contribution to the strength of the national economy. In 1999–2000 they generated directly and indirectly over £34.8 billion of output and over 562,000 full time equivalent jobs throughout the economy. This is equivalent to 2.7 per cent of the UK workforce in employment. For every 100 jobs within the HEIs themselves, a further 89 were generated through knock-on effects throughout the economy; and for every £1 million of economic output from higher education, a further £1.5 million is generated in other sectors of the economy.[1]

1.6   **Research** in higher education has real strengths. Britain has produced 44 Nobel prize winners in the last 50 years. With 1 per cent of the world's population we have an 8 per cent share of the world's scientific publications. 13 per cent of the world's most highly cited publications are British, which shows that our research has a strong influence on other work.

---

1   'The impact of higher education institutions on the UK economy'; Universities UK (May 2002).

We score better than anyone in the world except the USA on each of these measures (Figure 1). And out of 20 main fields of scientific research, while the USA with its unsurpassed research base leads the field in each case, the UK has the second largest share of citations in 15 areas and comes no lower than fifth in any discipline. Collaborations with our European partners through the Framework programmes have already strengthened and extended our research base very significantly. UK science and technology have been major beneficiaries of EU funding. And 'Investing in Innovation', the Government's strategy for science, engineering and technology, announced significant increases in funding for research.

Figure 1: Number of world citations of scientific publications per country, 1981–2000

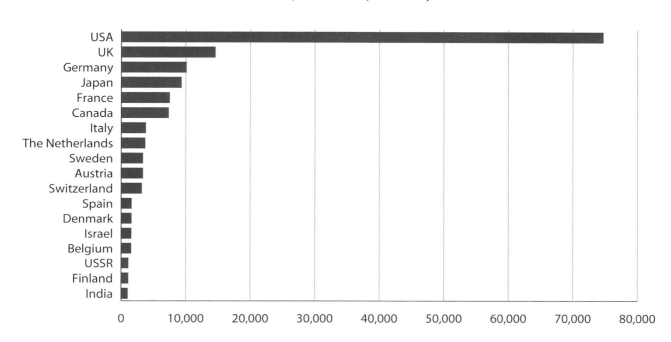

Source: Office of Science and Technology, 2002

1.7 Most students are satisfied with the standard of **teaching and learning**, and British higher education brings substantial benefits. Ninety-three per cent of full-time first-degree students are in employment or going on to further study six months after graduation. Those who have been through higher education in the UK earn on average 50 per cent more than those who have not,[2] and the rate of return from higher education in the UK is higher than in any other OECD country. Our non-completion rate for first degrees remains just 17 per cent, which is almost the lowest in the OECD. Britain is a growing and attractive destination in the highly competitive market for overseas students. In 1962–63 there were 28,000 overseas students in Great Britain, representing 8 per cent of the student population; by 2001–02 there were about 225,000, almost 11 per cent.

2   This includes 'sub-degree' higher education provision. For honours graduates, the figure is 64 per cent.

1.8 Links between universities and business are strong and growing. The record of our universities and colleges has been encouraging as measured by business start-ups and other spin out activity. During 2001, universities created 175 new spin-out companies, and that number has been increasing rapidly – it averaged around 70 a year in the five years to 1999–2000.[3] They include innovative companies like the Leeds spin-out Ecertec, which aims to develop smart materials that will allow, for example, 'warpable' wings to change shape on aircraft. There has also been a sharp increase in the number of patents filed, up 22 per cent between 1998–99 and 1999–2000, and the proportion of higher education research income funded by companies in the UK is also up and is now at a higher level than even the USA. There are numerous examples of higher education institutions helping companies to be more innovative and competitive. For example, Exeter University provides product development facilities which have assisted more than 300 small firms. And institutions now offer a wide range of courses to provide continuing professional development to employees in specific firms or business sectors. Higher education also plays a key role in supporting knowledge transfer and innovation management in the public sector – for example, in the NHS.

1.9 Our system has successfully transformed itself from an elite system – in which, in 1962, only around 6 per cent those under 21[4] participated – to one where in England around 43 per cent of those aged between 18 and 30 go to university. Despite the rise in the numbers participating in higher education, the average salary premium has not declined over time and remains the highest in the OECD.[5] It is not the case that 'more means worse'.

1.10 At the same time universities have changed the nature of their provision to reflect the changing demands of students. Some higher education institutions have gone out of their way to encourage applications from schools and colleges whose students do not normally participate. Others have embraced new ways of delivering learning and new types of course to meet the needs of a wider range of learners. The number of students receiving qualifications below degree level grew by 39 per cent between 1994–95 and 2001–02, far faster than the increase in the numbers receiving honours degrees (up by 12 per cent). Part-time study, where students can combine learning with work, is expanding too, with 11 per cent of first degree graduates obtaining their qualification through part-time study, compared to 10 per cent in 1994–95.[6] Eleven per cent of higher education students are studying in Further Education Colleges, allowing them to learn near home or work, and providing progression paths through from earlier study. In 2000/01 21 per cent of students studied from home, compared to 15 per cent in 1994–95.

---

3   Survey by UK Universities Companies Association (UNICO) and Nottingham University Business School (2002); and "Higher Education – business interaction survey", a report by the Centre for urban and regional development studies, Newcastle upon Tyne.

4   Based on the API measure, of the proportion of 18 year olds entering HE by the age of 20.

5   OECD, Education at a Glance 2002.

6   The figure for 2001–02 comes from a DfES Statistical First Release published in January 2003.

The danger of decline

1.11 Higher education in England therefore has a good story to tell. Nonetheless, the whole system is undoubtedly under severe pressure and at serious risk of decline. Decisions must be taken now to maintain the excellence of the sector as a whole.

1.12 The challenges are clear. Many of our economic competitors invest more in higher education institutions than we do. France, Germany, the Netherlands and the USA all contribute 1 per cent of GDP in public funding to higher education institutions, and Japan is planning to increase public investment from 0.4 per cent to 1 per cent. This compares to 0.8 per cent in the UK, rising to approximately 0.9 per cent by 2005 because of our generous spending review settlement.[7] Our competitors see – as we should – that the developing knowledge economy means the need for more, better trained people in the workforce. And higher education is becoming a global business. Our competitors are looking to sell higher education overseas, into the markets we have traditionally seen as ours.

1.13 There are challenges internal to higher education here too:

- to recruit, retain and reward the calibre of academic staff needed to sustain and improve both teaching and research.

- to maintain the infrastructure for research and teaching.

- to make sure the investment in higher education – whether paid for by the taxpayer, the student, their employer or someone else – is used to best effect.

RESEARCH

1.14 There is a real danger that our current strength in the world will not be maintained. The Research Assessment Exercise, in which research funding through the Higher Education Funding Council for England (HEFCE) is distributed according to quality and volume of research, has undoubtedly led to an overall increase in quality over the last 15 years. But there is growing competition from other countries. Looking at Nobel prizes, or at citation rates for scientists, indicates that although our position is still strong it is declining. And we may not be making the best use of inevitably limited research funds at home. International comparisons show that other countries, like Germany, the Netherlands and the USA (where research and the award of research degrees is confined to 200 out of 1600 'four year' institutions) concentrate their research in relatively few institutions. Similarly, the Chinese Government is planning to concentrate research

---

7   These figures relate to spending on Higher Education institutions, and do not include student support. The figure for 2005 is an estimate which might vary depending on the rate of growth in GDP.

funds through the creation of ten world-class universities; and in India there is a national Institute of Technology, on five sites across the country. This suggests we need to look again at how our research is organised, and make sure we capture the benefits of concentration, and that we have a number of institutions able to compete with the best in the world.

1.15 The Transparency Review, which looked for the first time at the distribution of expenditure on research and teaching in HEIs across the UK, showed that research was under-funded, and the deficit was made up at the expense of investment in the research infrastructure, or of teaching.[8] The effect was particularly marked in institutions which were not research-intensive. Approximately half of the higher education estate was built, to relatively low and inflexible specifications, in the 1960s and early 1970s. Much of it is nearing the end of its design life, and new requirements arise from scientific and technological advance, as well as recent growth in research volumes. The reports commissioned from JM Consulting by HEFCE[9] found that there was an infrastructure backlog of about £8 billion, consisting of a research infrastructure backlog of £3.2 billion, and a teaching infrastructure backlog of £4.6 billion, plus a need to double spending on maintenance.

1.16 And there are continuing concerns about our ability to recruit, retain and reward the best researchers who provide the essential research leadership. Although the overall figures show a 'brain-gain' rather than a 'brain-drain' in flows of scientists into and out of the country, figures from the Royal Society support the hypothesis that the researchers moving out of the country – typically to the USA – are among our best. A survey of Royal Society Fellows found that in 1999 26 per cent of Fellows worked outside the UK (12 per cent in the USA). We need to consider how to attract and retain the best researchers internationally, and how to maintain a steady flow of the brightest and best young people into research.

1.17 Average earnings have risen considerably faster than academic pay over the last 20 years. Comparing USA and UK academic salaries, it is striking that the difference in average salary scales is far smaller than the difference in salaries at the top end, for the best researchers. This raises questions about whether our institutions are using salaries to the best possible effect in recruiting and retaining excellent rsearchers. International comparisons suggest we should also be thinking hard about whether institutions could do more to help the best researchers focus on research, rather than teaching and administrative duties.

---

8   Investing in Innovation – A strategy for science, engineering and technology (July 2002).
9   Study of Science Research Infrastructure, Report to OST, March 2002, and Teaching and Learning Infrastructure in Higher Education, Report to the HEFCE by JM Consulting, June 2002 .

TEACHING

1.18 Teaching has for too long been the poor relation in higher education. Promotion for academics is based largely on research excellence, rather than teaching ability. There is no respected and defined separate professional career track for higher education teaching in its own right. Only around 12 per cent of academic staff in higher education are members of the Institute for Learning and Teaching in Higher Education, and not all of those necessarily have any formal teaching qualification. And here again there are recruitment difficulties. HEFCE's annual survey[10] reveals a recruitment situation that has steadily deteriorated since the survey was inaugurated in 1998. Over 60 per cent of institutions reported difficulties in recruiting lecturers. Recruitment difficulties were particularly concentrated in certain subjects, notably computing/IT, business-related subjects, science, engineering, medicine-related subjects and education.

1.19 Students have insufficient information on how good the teaching is when applying for courses. And here again there is a story of decline: staff-student ratios have fallen from just over 1:10 in 1983 to 1:18 in 2000 and this tends to mean that students write fewer assignments and have less face-to-face contact with staff.[11] There is too little collaboration between higher education institutions (HEIs), which can raise standards; support the development of modules and courses particularly at the introductory level; and promote the innovative use of ICT and credit accumulation and transfer.

HE AND BUSINESS

1.20 The proportion of businesses using information from HEIs to help with innovation has increased over recent years, and is now 16 per cent of companies. But this is still a small minority.[12] When universities were asked to benchmark themselves, fewer than half declared that they had more than a restricted or partially implemented plan for business support.[13] A succession of employer surveys reveals concerns about the skills of graduates, particularly in terms of communication and other 'soft' skills. And although UK institutions are growing stronger in knowledge transfer, their exploitation of intellectual property – to take one example – is weak by international standards.[14]

1.21 These weaknesses are not all of HEIs' making. Universities have often experienced difficulties in transferring knowledge to business through research and development work, and businesses are often unclear about what they want. And, though the new Regional Development Agencies are now building graduate-level skills into their planning, this is in many cases a relatively recent development. There is clearly scope for the higher education

---

10 Recruitment and Retention of Staff in UK higher education 2001, HEFCE.

11 cf. Evidence in Independent Review of Higher Education Pay and Conditions, 1999.

12 Community Innovation Survey; DTI (2001).

13 HE Business Interaction Survey; HEFCE (2001).

14 Research expenditure per patent in the UK is almost double that in the USA and Canada – *Higher education-business interaction survey*; A report by the Centre for Urban and Regional Development Studies, University of Newcastle upon Tyne (2001), table 5.7.

sector to improve its performance still further and for businesses to be clearer about what they want from HEIs. This will be informed by the outcome of the Lambert review, announced by the Chancellor of the Exchequer in November 2002, which will investigate ways in which the interactions between universities and businesses can be enhanced.

EXPANSION AND FLEXIBILITY

1.22 Demand for graduates is very strong, and research shows that 80 per cent of the 1.7 million new jobs which are expected to be created by the end of the decade will be in occupations which normally recruit those with higher education qualifications.[15] So it is in the country's interest to expand higher education. At the moment we calculate that the participation rate for English students in higher education is around 43 per cent of 18–30 year olds.[16] Participation rates are lower, according to OECD comparisons, than in many other developed countries, including Australia, Finland, the Netherlands, New Zealand, Norway and Sweden.

1.23 There is even more catching up to do when we look at education levels in the existing workforce, rather than at current entry rates. The proportion of the whole labour force educated to degree level in the UK is 17 per cent compared to 28 per cent in the USA.[17]

1.24 If we want to close the productivity gap we must close the skills gap, and that in part means boosting higher education. But we are also convinced that expansion should not mean more of the same. The pace of both social and technological change means that education, including higher education, can no longer be confined to the early years of life. This is truly an era of lifelong learning. Today's generation of students will need to return to learning – full-time or part-time – on more that one occasion across their lifetime in order to refresh their knowledge, upgrade their skills and sustain their employability. Such independent learners investing in the continuous improvement of their skills will underpin innovation and enterprise in the economy and society. Lifelong learning therefore implies a fundamental shift from the 'once in a lifetime' approach to higher education to one of educational progression linked to a process of continuous personal and professional development.

1.25 There is good evidence to suggest that the skills gap is most acute at a level that is represented by higher education qualifications below degree level, particularly two-year work-focused provision. The National Skills Task Force reported that jobs in the 'associate professional' and higher technician level will experience the greatest growth in the coming years, increasing by 790,000 up to 2010. And analysis of the Employer Skills Survey 2002 shows that associate professionals and technical occupations have the highest proportion of skill shortage vacancies relative to the numbers employed – 1.2 per cent compared to 0.2 per cent for managers. Shorter, more work-focused courses are also better suited to a culture of continuous professional development.

15 Wilson, R.A., and A. E. Green (2001). Projections of Occupations and Qualifications: 2000/2001: Research in Support of the National Skills Taskforce. Sheffield: Department for Education and Employment.

16 For English domiciled students in UK HE.

17 Source: OECD, Education at a Glance 2002.

1.26 Work-focused courses at these levels have suffered from social and cultural prejudice against vocational education. Employers claim that they want graduates whose skills are better fitted for work; but the labour market premium they pay still favours traditional three-year honours degrees over two-year work-focused ones. And students have therefore continued to apply for three-year honours courses in preference. We must break this cycle of low esteem, to offer attractive choices to students about the types of course they can undertake.

1.27 And this is true not just of work-focused provision. Our system is not good enough at offering students real choice about how they learn. Higher education should be a choice open to everyone with the potential to benefit – including older people in the workforce who want to update their skills. There are not enough choices for flexible study – including part-time courses, sandwich courses, distance learning, and e-learning – and there must be an increasingly rich variety of subjects to study, which keep pace with changes in society and the economy.

FAIR ACCESS TO HIGHER EDUCATION

1.28 Universities are a vital gateway to opportunity and fulfilment for young people, so it is crucial that they continue to make real and sustained improvements in **access**. The social class gap among those entering higher education is unacceptably wide. Those from the top three social classes are almost three times as likely to enter higher education as those from the bottom three. Figure 2, below, is even more disturbing, because it shows that the gap has widened. At the extremes, the picture is worse. Young people from professional backgrounds are over five times more likely to enter higher education than those from unskilled backgrounds.

Figure 2: Higher Education entrants by social class groups (1960–2000)

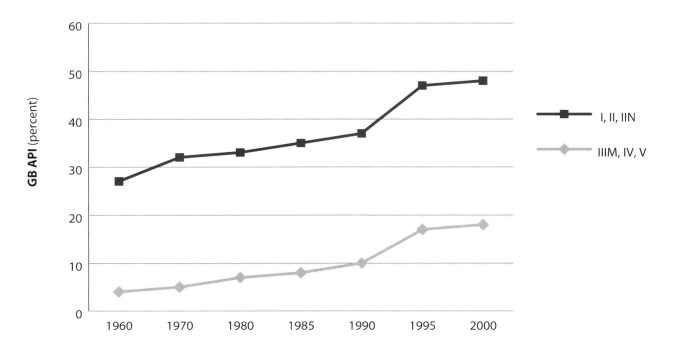

1.29 This state of affairs cannot be tolerated in a civilised society. It wastes our national talent; and it is inherently socially unjust. We know that the roots of inequality are deep – in the education system, social class differences show themselves from the very earliest years. We are tackling them throughout the education system and beyond, knowing that the most important factor in getting access to higher education is earlier results at school or college. But we cannot allow this to be an excuse for failing to take decisive action to improve access to higher education. We must do everything that can be done to make sure that everyone who has the potential to benefit from a university education has the opportunity to do so.

1.30 And our access difficulties occur despite having a level of public spending on financial aid to students (including student loans) as a percentage of total public expenditure on higher education that is the highest in the OECD – 36 per cent in the UK, compared with 8 per cent in France, 19 per cent in Canada and 30 per cent in Sweden.

FUNDING

1.31 Underlying each of these policy challenges is a funding challenge. The graph below (figure 3) shows that although publicly planned funding for higher education has risen dramatically under this Government, the decline in the unit of funding was only reversed in 2000–01. We saw a drop of 36 per cent in funding per student between 1989 and 1997.[18] We have outlined, above, the funding challenges that come from wanting a world-class research operation; and we know that there is an infrastructure backlog in both teaching and research.

Figure 3: Comparison of Total Publicly Planned funding for Higher Education (£million) and Unit funding (£) (1989–2003)

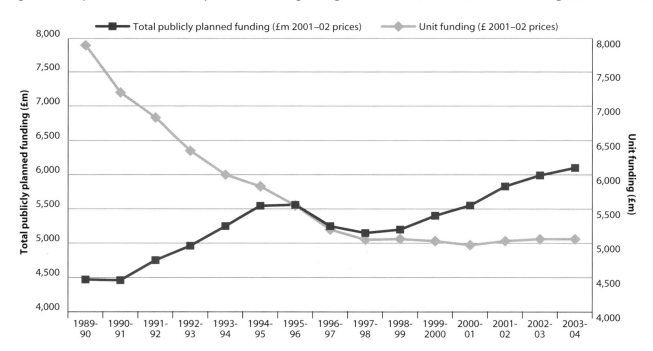

18 For full-time equivalent students.

1.32 The Government has committed substantial investment to education. Between 1997 and 2006, the proportion of GDP spent on education will rise from 4.5 per cent to 5.6 per cent. Spending on higher education will rise from a total of around £7.5 billion in 2002–03 to almost £10 billion in 2005–06 – a real terms increase of over 6 per cent each year. The table below gives an outline of how the money will be used.

Summary of the Spending Review Settlement for Higher Education in England (£million)

	02–03	03–04	04–05	05–06	per cent Increase in in cash terms 05–06 over 02–03
Research*	1,910	2,144	2,318	2,633	38
of which capital*	256	364	453	453	77
Knowledge transfer*	62	82	101	114	84
Teaching and learning	3,943	4,230	4,604	4,963	26
of which capital	155	207	377	442	185
Expansion	0	9	21	32	
Access and widening particpation	86	119	130	132	53
Management, leadership, and					
strategic development	15	23	32	34	127
Student support**	1,578	1,691	1,839	1,996	26
Other	2	11	12	14	
Total recurrent	*7,185*	*7,738*	*8,227*	*9,023*	
Total capital	*411*	*571*	*830*	*895*	
Grand Total	7,596	8,309	9,057	9,918	31

* Including estimates of the amount of the Office of Science and Technology's UK wide funding that is likely to go to HE institutions in England. These estimates are forward projections based on spending in previous years by OST and the OST Research Councils.

** Estimated share of student support likely to go on HE student domiciled in England. These estimates are based on the most recent data from the Student Loans Company.

1.33 This allocation is the most generous for a decade. It will stabilise the funding of universities, and allow them to make sustained progress in improving research volumes and quality and in tackling the huge backlogs in research and teaching infrastructure.

1.34 The Government will continue to stand by universities in future spending review settlements. However, for our universities to be able to develop their strengths and address the challenges that the future will bring requires a more sustainable funding regime with greater freedom for them to be able to access new funding streams on their own account.

1.35 In the long term, we see a much greater role for universities establishing endowment funds and using the income from them, in much the same way as is done in the United States. For example, Harvard has an endowment fund of $18 billion, while Oxford University and its colleges have only £2 billion. This, though, will require a significant change in attitude from donors, including alumni. Each year approximately 10 per cent of Princeton University's overall budget is raised through Annual Giving. In 1999–2000, Annual Giving produced a record $35.7 million in unrestricted funds, with 60.8 per cent of all former undergraduate alumni participating. Durham University's Annual Giving Programme, which has grown considerably in recent years, has only raised a total of somewhere over £1.5 million since 1994. If we are to give them real freedom, we must look at ways of helping our universities change the culture of giving and lever in more funding of their own.

1.36 We also believe it is right that individual universities should be able to secure increased contributions from their graduates to supplement the substantial support that they receive from the taxpayer, subject to firm limits to protect access and fairness. Different courses and universities bring different benefits to graduates, and we think that it is right both that universities should get differential benefits, and that graduates should make differential contributions to reflect that.

DIVERSITY AND MISSION

1.37 The sector has embraced lifelong learning, research, knowledge transfer, social inclusion and regional economic development. There is a broad consensus within higher education that all of these elements are both welcome and necessary. However, it is unreasonable to expect all higher education institutions to sustain all of these activities simultaneously at global, and not just national, levels of excellence. No higher education system in the world is organised in this way. Rather, scarce resources are applied in such a way as to produce a focus on comparative advantage: individual institutions focus on what they do best, while the sector as a whole achieves this much wider range of objectives.

1.38 There is already a great deal of diversity within the sector. But it needs to be acknowledged and celebrated, with institutions both openly identifying and playing to their strengths.

1.39 The Government accepts that it has been partly responsible for the failure to have an honest recognition of universities' different roles. For example, institutions have in large measure been driven towards greater involvement in research by the incentives in the funding mechanisms, and by the criteria for being awarded the status of a university (which helps them recruit students). Government will continue to be the principal funder of higher education, but we need to move to a funding regime which enables each institution to choose its mission and the funding streams necessary to support it, and to make sure that our system recognises and celebrates different missions properly.

1.40 We also see a strong link between the development of stronger missions and growing collaboration in the sector. One of the results of universities acting as if they all had the same mission has been that institutions across the sector view each other as competitors; more diversity will make collaboration easier as institutions with complementary missions associate.

In research, this will help us preserve the best pockets of isolated research while concentrating funding on the very best; in teaching, it will help the spreading of good practice and the development of seamless progression routes for students; and in linking with business it will help make sure that groups of institutions can be responsive to a wide range of business needs.

1.41 Both mission and collaboration are challenges that will demand outstanding management and leadership in our higher education institutions. We must support the sector in developing the capacity not only to manage these changes, but also to be in the driving seat of future reform.

The vision for higher education

1.42 We cannot shirk the challenge of these critical issues. Higher education is too important. Our spending review settlement for the next three years is generous, and allows us to take the first steps towards our new vision for higher education. But we must use it to do more than hold off decline. We must take this opportunity to lay the foundations for the reforms which will transform the future of the sector.

1.43 Realising our vision will take time. Having presented a radical picture of a freer future, it is the duty of government to make sure that the transition is managed carefully and sensibly so that change is not destabilising. So in some areas government will want to support the way in which institutions move towards new freedoms, and develop new patterns of provision. Government also has to retain a role because it is the only body that can balance competing interests between the different stakeholders. It will also have a responsibility to intervene when universities fail to provide adequate opportunities or when access, quality or standards are at risk.

1.44 We see a higher education sector which meets the needs of the economy in terms of trained people, research, and technology transfer. At the same time it needs to enable all suitably qualified individuals to develop their potential both intellectually and personally, and to provide the necessary storehouse of expertise in science and technology, and the arts and humanities which defines our civilisation and culture.

1.45 To do so, our vision is of a sector which:

- recognises and values universities as creators of knowledge and understanding and as engines for applying that new knowledge for the benefit of all;

- recognises their role in educating their students to live life to the full, through the acquisition of skills and through fostering imagination, creativity and contribution to society;

- acknowledges and celebrates the differences between institutions as each defines and implements its own mission. We see all HEIs excelling in teaching and reaching out to low participation groups, coupled with strengths in one or more of: research; knowledge transfer; linking to the local and regional economy; and providing clear opportunities for students to progress;

- builds strong and purposeful collaborations, including with one another and with further education, to support the best teaching, research management and knowledge transfer;

- supports and celebrates institutions which can compete with the best in the world in research;

- is expanding towards 50 per cent participation for young people aged 18–30 years from all backgrounds and providing courses which satisfy both students and employers;

- meets the developing needs of students for new modes of study and delivery of courses as well as pastoral and learning support;

- offers the opportunity of higher education to all those who have the potential to benefit;

- employs sufficient staff of the right calibre to achieve its missions, and which recruits, develops, retains and rewards them adequately;

- has the freedom to be innovative and entrepreneurial, with strong management and visionary leadership which will set and achieve clear goals for improving quality across the whole range of each institution's activity to implement its plans; and

- has sufficient funding from a range of sources to sustain the sector and the institutions within it, and with an equitable partnership for investment in higher education shared between the taxpayer, the student and others.

1.46 This document sets out our strategy to move towards that vision. We are confident that greater explicit differentiation, greater freedom and greater collaboration are the keys to delivering the further improvement in quality we shall need to retain and strengthen our position as one of the world's leading higher education systems.

Chapter 2
Research excellence – building on our strengths

Reform

Research lays the long-term foundations for innovation, which is central to improved growth, productivity and quality of life. This applies not only to scientific and technical knowledge. Research in the social sciences, and in the arts and humanities can also benefit the economy – for example, in tourism, social and economic trends, design, law, and the performing arts – not to speak of enriching our culture more widely. In addition, the strong research base in the UK helps us to take advantage of research conducted elsewhere. It provides the expertise to keep up with international developments, and the clout to join international partnerships. But competition is fierce. The USA, Japan, Canada, and other nations are significantly increasing their investment in research. To maintain our position and build on our generous Spending Review settlement, we need to think carefully about how research is organised and funded.

Key points and proposals

■ The recent spending review will increase expenditure on science and research in 2005–06 by £1.25 billion a year compared to 2002–03 – around 30 per cent in real terms.

■ We want to think carefully about the way research funding is managed and distributed, so that it works in the most effective way. To do this, we will take three important steps:

  – We propose to encourage the formation of consortia, provide extra funding for research in larger, better managed research units, and develop criteria to judge the strength of collaborative work.

  – As part of this process, we will invest even more in our very best research institutions, enabling them to compete effectively with the world's best universities.

  – And we will also make sure that the very best individual departments are not neglected, by making a clearer distinction between the strong and the strongest.

■ It is important that new research areas and centres can emerge and flourish. We will support emerging and improving research and make sure that the system does not ossify.

- We will invest in developing and rewarding talented researchers. There will be rigorous new standards for government-funded research postgraduate places, and good researchers will be rewarded, through the extra investment in research in general, money earmarked for pay, and more time to concentrate on research.

- We will create a UK wide Arts and Humanities Research Council, to put the organisation of funding for the arts and humanities on the same footing as funding for science and technology.

- Our proposals build on the Government's strategy for science, engineering and technology, "Investing in Innovation", published in July 2002.

Research funding

2.1   Chapter 1 sets out our record of quality and productivity in research, and the central role that our universities play in it. But as more countries seek to emulate this performance and increase their investment in research, the competition intensifies. We cannot stand still if we are to sustain the excellence and international standing of research in our universities. That is why, last July, the Government published its strategy for the UK science base, 'Investing in Innovation'.[19] Building on the increased funding for research in science and technology since 1998, part of which has begun the long overdue restoration of the research infrastructure, there will be a further increase of £1.25 billion by 2005–06 compared to 2002–03, around 30 per cent in real terms. But to maintain and strengthen our position in the face of increasing global competition, we also need to review how research is organised to ensure the increased funding supports our most talented researchers and our most effective research institutions and departments.

2.2   Core public funding for higher education research is provided through the 'dual support system' – one stream via HEFCE to support the underpinning research capability of institutions, which is distributed selectively according to the quality of research as measured by the Research Assessment Exercise (RAE). The other stream flows via the research councils and the Arts and Humanities Research Board to support specific research projects.

2.3   The Government's increased level of investment in research was announced last July in the document 'Investing in Innovation'. Box A below gives the main points.

---

19 It can be found on the Treasury website, at www.hm-treasury.gov.uk/Spending_Review.

BOX A: INVESTING IN INNOVATION: KEY ANNOUNCEMENTS

- A £244 million increase, compared with plans for 2002–03, in the money available to the Higher Education Funding Council for England for the research component of university block grants.

- A substantial and dedicated stream of capital for universities, worth £500 million per year by 2004–05, to develop their science research infrastructure and to allow them to plan for their future with certainty.

- Universities to put in place systems to ensure and demonstrate that their research is financially sustainable.

- an extra £120 million for the research councils from 2005–06 to enable them to make a more realistic contribution to the full costs of the research that they sponsor in universities.

- Increased basic research through sustained real annual growth of 5 per cent in funding for research council programmes and equipment.

- An additional £50 million per year by 2005–06 to support collaborative research and development on key emerging and pervasive technologies such as nanotechnology, which looks at developing microscopically small objects, using individual atoms and molecules.

- Steps to improve the pay and training of scientific postgraduate researchers, and to enhance technology, mathematics and science education in schools, colleges and universities.

- Expansion of the Higher Education Innovation Fund, with funding to stimulate enterprise from research across the regions, to £90 million per year by 2005–06.

2.4 By historic standards, these are very significant investments, particularly when put alongside earlier schemes to renew the research infrastructure. This extra money will ensure that research projects are fully funded, so that universities do not have to cross-subsidise research from teaching, or scrimp on investment in infrastructure. The funding will also ensure that the current poor state of the research infrastructure in universities can be brought up to standard – because in many subjects good research increasingly depends on high-quality facilities and equipment. In return, universities will need to demonstrate that they are operating sustainable research businesses through recovering the full economic costs of research. Other research funders will also need to play their part.

Organisation of research

2.5   This increase in resources for research has been widely welcomed. The challenge now is to make best use of the money by making sure that research funding is allocated, organised and managed effectively. Recurrent funding for research is already distributed selectively, based on the outcome of the RAE, which judges the quality of research in departments. Details of the RAE are given in Box B, below.

2.6   The selectivity of research funding is illustrated by looking at RAE ratings, which mean that about 75 per cent of HEFCE research funding goes to the top 25 institutions, and research council grant funding follows a similar pattern. This means that some institutions have a high concentration of top quality research. But at the same time there is also a wide spread of individual departments in other universities undertaking high quality research – beyond the top 25, a further 52 institutions have at least one department rated 5 or 5* in the 2001 RAE, and departments rated 4 are yet more widespread. The issue is how best to balance four issues:

- rewarding research intensive institutions adequately;

- protecting relatively isolated pockets of high-quality research in institutions which are not themselves research intensive;

- encouraging and developing emerging areas of research; and

- steering non-research-intensive institutions towards other parts of their mission, and rewarding them properly for it, so that the RAE can be focused on the best research .

BOX B: THE RESEARCH ASSESSMENT EXERCISE

The Research Assessment Exercise (RAE) was introduced in 1986 as a way of selectively funding research according to defined quality standards. The RAE took place every four or five years through a process of peer review by panels of experts – both academics and users of research such as business people. The most recent RAE took place in 2001.

Institutions were able to submit their research in up to 69 different subject areas and each submission was awarded a quality rating according to a standard scale.

Rating	Description
5* (5 star)	Quality that equates to attainable levels of international excellence in more than half of the research activity submitted and attainable levels of national excellence in the remainder.
5	Quality that equates to attainable levels of international excellence in up to half of the research activity submitted and to attainable levels of national excellence in virtually all of the remainder.
4	Quality that equates to attainable levels of national excellence in virtually all of the research activity submitted, showing some evidence of international excellence.
3a	Quality that equates to attainable levels of national excellence in over two thirds of the research activity submitted, possibly showing evidence of international excellence.
3b	Quality that equates to attainable levels of national excellence in more than half of the research activity submitted.
2	Quality that equates to attainable levels of national excellence in up to half of the research activity submitted.
1	Quality that equates to attainable levels of national excellence in none, or virtually none, of the research activity submitted.

The rating, together with the volume of research associated with it, is an important variable in the formula used by HEFCE and the other higher education funding bodies to determine the funding allocations to institutions.

In 2002 the higher education funding bodies announced a wide ranging review of research assessment, chaired by Sir Gareth Roberts. This review will report later in 2003 and is likely to lead to a revised system of research assessment based on expert review and featuring research centres and partnerships of international standing.

2.7   We believe that the time has come to look carefully at the relationship between research and teaching. In reality, the connection between an institution's research activities and its teaching is indirect, and there is ample evidence of the highest quality teaching being achieved in circumstances which are not research-intensive. The scale and location of research activity has to be justified and decided on its own merits. We are also determined to promote other sources of recognition, achievement and prestige besides eminence in research, both within and between institutions, as set out elsewhere in this paper.

2.8   The Government intends to improve the position of research further by focusing resources more effectively on the best research performers, and by providing appropriate incentives for university researchers to collaborate among institutions and across traditional disciplines. Concentration brings real benefits, including better infrastructure (funding excellent equipment and good libraries), better opportunities for interdisciplinary research, and the benefits for both staff and students which flow from discussing their research and collaborating in projects. Modern research is less amenable to the 'lone scholar' model – for example, one study found that by 1994, 88 per cent of all UK HEI papers involved two or more authors and 55 per cent involved two or more institutions.[20] Furthermore, larger groups of researchers in a subject, or in related subjects, perform particularly well – at least in the natural and social sciences.[21] Greater concentration of resources also makes it easier to develop research only posts and to offer better pay to attract excellent researchers. As Chapter 1 points out, international comparisons – not only with the USA, but also with emerging competitors like China and India – suggest that we should be thinking hard about funding our research in larger, more concentrated units.

2.9   Collaboration is a way of life for many researchers. They see the benefits which flow from economies of scale and scope in terms of facilities, and from the sharing of knowledge and the more effective generation of new ideas. And, crucially, they know it allows excellent researchers, wherever they may be, to participate in the best research across the sector. Well-conceived collaborations:

■ will allow more intensive use of expensive plant and equipment;

■ will provide a higher proportion of unallocated funding which can be used to support speculative research, before it is ready for research council or other support. This unallocated funding would no longer have to be found at the expense of other activities as it is now in some non-research-intensive institutions;

■ can promote new and emerging areas of research;

20 *Collaborative Approaches to Research*, Smith D. and Katz J.S. (2000).
21 *The Role of Selectivity and the Characteristics of Excellence*, HE Policy Unit, University of Leeds (2000).

- share expertise for managing intellectual property and making the best use of patents (for example); and

- can ensure that good quality research in isolated pockets finds secure funding.

2.10 Some of these points are equally valid for the arts and humanities as for science and technology.

A framework for research development

2.11 Collaboration should be encouraged, and in a way which reinforces the benefits which it brings when it is done well. But it cannot be imposed top-down. So we do not have a blueprint for particular sorts of collaboration – we want to encourage them to grow organically over time.

2.12 We therefore intend to reward research that is more concentrated and better-managed, without being directive about the precise shape and formation of those collaborations, and without cutting off funding from others in the sector. The collaborations could take many forms, including:

- graduate schools to give high quality research training, and where 'Investing in Innovation' has already recommended HEFCE funding for research students should be dependent on meeting a set of strict quality criteria;

- within large cities or other areas collaborative units for example between departments in research-intensive and less research-intensive universities, possibly linked to collaborations in teaching and knowledge transfer as well;

- within regions, formal research partnerships where there is added value by combining strengths (see Box C below);

- in certain areas, and where this is appropriate, forming powerful clusters of research between universities, government laboratories, research council laboratories or units, and units funded by charities.

2.13 In each case the central issue will be whether the arrangements add value in terms of improving the quality of research or graduate training. Where institutions already have great individual strength and depth in research across the board, there is no merit in forcing collaboration or cooperation just for the sake of it. Nevertheless, this approach would reward research concentration and synergy, and encourage appropriate collaboration between institutions. We know that these issues are being examined by Sir Gareth Roberts as part of his review of research assessment, and we envisage these arrangements, or similar ones, folding into his proposals in the longer term. But we ought to begin to capture the benefits earlier. To do this, we propose to ask HEFCE, in consultation with Office for Science and Technology (OST), to provide funding which will incentivise the formation of productive collaborations through initial pump-priming.

BOX C: THE WHITE ROSE CONSORTIUM

The White Rose Consortium is an association of the three major research universities in Yorkshire – Leeds, Sheffield and York, and has a large critical mass of research, teaching, and enterprise facilities. It has developed a number of collaborative projects, including a Bioscience partnership which has been highly successful in realising the economic benefits of university research. The partnership has created 21 spin-out companies, signed 14 technology licences and filed more than 40 patents in areas such as healthcare, bioinformatics and plant sciences.

Research Assessment

2.14 HEFCE (together with the equivalent bodies in the devolved administrations) is undertaking a review of research assessment which will investigate different approaches to the definition and evaluation of research quality, drawing on the lessons of both the recent RAE and other models of research assessment. The review is now under way, and has consulted widely within the sector and with other stakeholders. The responses show overwhelming support for the continued use of expert review and considerable support for reducing the numbers of units of assessment. The need to recognise multi-disciplinary research activity and collaborative research fully has also been endorsed. The revised research assessment exercise to be introduced, probably in 2008–09, is therefore likely to grade broader subject groupings than before and also recognise centres of excellence. Such indicators will enable the community to identify and designate leading research institutions. The report on the Review of Research Assessment will be submitted to the UK funding councils in April 2003.

2.15 We welcome these likely outcomes. However, a further Research Assessment Exercise is not due until 2008, and we believe that there is a case for more discrimination between the best before then. In the last RAE, 55 per cent of research active staff were in departments rated 5 or 5*. We will ask HEFCE, using the results of the latest Research Assessment Exercise, along with international peer review of additional material, to identify the very best of the 5* departments which have a critical mass of researchers – a "6*" – and will provide additional resources to give them an uplift in funding over the next three years. At subject as well as at institutional level, it is critical that we focus our resources on the strongest, who bring us the best returns.

2.16 Once the review is complete, HEFCE will need to do further work to design a funding system which fits effectively with this new system of assessment. We must be sure that the new system can be fully funded from within the resources available. And in all this, HEFCE will want to consider how to put these principles into practice while keeping bureaucracy to a minimum.

Supporting our leading universities

2.17 The best universities contain a critical mass of research groups which can compete globally in a wide range of disciplines. But – as noted above – the increasing competition from overseas means we cannot assume they will remain at the cutting edge. We need to consider what else needs to be done if we are to continue to retain our leading position. The increase in research funding overall, the designation and reward for a new category of research departments, and our extra support for larger units will certainly help our leading research institutions to recruit and retain the staff they need.

2.18 However, increased funding on its own is not enough to ensure these institutions can stay at the cutting edge. They also need the leadership, governance and management to put in place outstanding research planning, sound policies with respect to intellectual property, and a willingness to collaborate with others, and to help exploit the knowledge they generate. The Lambert Review of links between higher education and business will ask business for its views on the present governance, management and leadership arrangements and their effectiveness in supporting good research and knowledge transfer and providing relevant skills for the economy.

2.19 Where they have these arrangements in place in addition to the critical mass of excellent research, we will allocate additional capital funding to allow them additional flexibility to achieve their institutional goals for research. This will mean that as a nation we continue to reap the social and economic benefits of being at the forefront of the world in science and technology. Our best research will be explicitly recognised, as well as properly funded. There will be regular reassessments so that as strong new institutions and consortia develop they can also be recognised as leading institutions; and so that institutions which cannot maintain their leading status are not sustained on the basis of reputation alone.

Supporting Emerging Research

2.20 Though it is right to focus resources on the best, we must also make sure that the allocation of funding overall encourages and rewards promising departments with comparatively low research ratings, particularly for work in new research areas, so that they have the resources to develop and improve.

2.21 In order to do this, we will ask HEFCE to look at how funding for departments with lower ratings under the existing system can be related to potential to progress further, and linked to good planning for future improvement. This needs to go alongside the identification and funding of emerging and potentially important areas of research in order to build capacity in disciplines that are strategically important. We are asking HEFCE to take the first steps in 2003.

The Creation of an Arts and Humanities Research Council

2.22 Research in the arts and humanities is of vital importance to our university system and its international standing. At present, research in the arts and humanities is funded by the Arts and Humanities Research Board (AHRB) (as well as through HEFCE), rather than by a research council. In September 2001, the Government and devolved administrations launched a review of arts and humanities funding. The aim of the review was to enhance provision of arts and humanities research, and to ensure that there are no artificial barriers to interdisciplinary work between the arts and sciences, as well as to make sure that the arts and humanities are properly resourced and supported.

2.23 This review concluded that the AHRB should take on the status of a fully fledged research council funded by the Office of Science and Technology in the same way as the other research councils. This recommendation will be put into action as the legislative timetable allows, with the aim of achieving a fully functioning, statutory research council by 2005. We expect the benefits to include stronger links between researchers in different disciplines, more participation by the arts and humanities in national and international programmes, and reduced bureaucracy for institutions as AHRC systems are aligned with those of the other research councils.

The Roberts Review of skilled people in science and technology

2.24 The Government last year asked Sir Gareth Roberts to undertake a review of the supply of people with science, technology, engineering and mathematics skills. The report of Sir Gareth's work, 'SET for success',[22] was published in April 2002. And the Government responded to Sir Gareth's report as part of the science strategy set out in 'Investing in Innovation'.

2.25 Sir Gareth's report emphasised the need for high-calibre PhD students – the academic or business researchers of tomorrow, and a key ingredient in our universities' future success. In order to attract the best students into postgraduate study, the Government has announced substantial increases in the stipend for research council funded PhD students – from the 2003–04 minimum of £9,000 to a £12,000 minimum by 2005–06, with more in shortage subjects to raise the average still higher.

22 This can also be found on the Treasury website at: www.hm-treasury.gov.uk/roberts.

2.26 The training of PhD students also merits close attention. The Roberts Review looked at the need for high standards of PhD work, adequate supervision of students, and training in transferable skills. As set out in 'Investing in Innovation', we will ask HEFCE to set high minimum standards for the training of PhD students which must be met before higher education institutions can draw down funding for PhD places, though they could still fund PhD places from their own resources if they wished to do so. This may lead to larger graduate schools in fewer HEIs, as some institutions decide not to offer PhD places, and others are in a position to play to their strengths in PhD training by expanding their postgraduate provision. In time, this might play into a model where postgraduate degree awarding powers are restricted to successful research consortia.

Investing in Researchers

2.27 Ensuring that pay rates and facilities for research leaders in the UK are competitive is essential. Institutions have specific additional support to attract and retain researchers of outstanding achievement and potential, through the Wolfson – OST Research Merit Awards. To secure the brightest and the best, universities must be able to pay the market rate, and we are making sure that they have the resources to do so, both through our overall funding proposals, and through our propositions on the concentration of research. Chapter 4 gives more details of our proposals on pay.

2.28 We will encourage institutions to establish more research-only posts, something which can help to attract and retain talented researchers. Good progress has been made here, and 4.1 per cent of UK lecturers were employed in research-only posts in 2000–01, compared to only 3.2 per cent in 1995–96. However, we still believe that more could be done to free up our best researchers, and as investment in research improves, we hope that this will become easier for those institutions wishing to concentrate on research.

2.29 But whilst research is led by outstanding researchers, their work depends in large measure on the efforts of others: academics, research students, and other research staff. Both the Roberts Report, and the more recent report by the House of Commons Science and Technology Committee on short-term research contracts in science and engineering, highlighted the need to do more to promote the recruitment, retention, training and career progression of junior researchers. Their knowledge and skills are vital to successful research programmes. In taking forward the recommendations in 'Investing in Innovation', the Office of Science and Technology and the Department for Education and Skills are also taking some specific steps to improve research careers and the rewards of research. These include:

- Providing funding to increase the average research council postdoctoral salary by around £4,000 by 2005–06;

- Improving the training available to research council funded postdoctoral researchers as well as to PhD students; and

- Creating 1,000 new academic fellowships over five years to provide more stable and attractive routes into academia.

2.30 It is for institutions to ensure that they recruit and retain the research staff they need, but we have made clear to HEFCE that support for junior research staff will be expected to feature in institutions' human resources strategies – including effective training and scope for career development. We will also take steps to ensure that mechanisms for funding and quality assessment do not inadvertently reinforce particular models for managing research staff. We expect the review of research assessment to consider the impact of its proposals on the work and career development of junior researchers.

2.31 New regulations to prevent the less favourable treatment of fixed-term employees came into force last year. These will help to improve conditions for contract research staff and will limit the use of successive short-term contracts, a particular problem for some researchers. The Government expects that a combination of this and the increased research funding announced in the spending review will enable institutions more flexibility to provide continuing employment for their staff.

2.32 To complement our proposals for identifying and funding promising or emerging areas of research, we will also introduce a Promising Researcher Fellowship Scheme which will provide funding for a talented researcher in a non-research-intensive department (scoring 4 or below in the RAE) to spend 6 months researching in a high-scoring department. The awards would be made to an individual, could be taken up in the researcher's own research cluster or elsewhere, and would be worth up to £50,000 for six months, including funding to replace the Fellow's teaching. We expect to provide funding to 100 people a year by 2004.

Conclusion

2.33 Taken together with the exceptionally generous funding settlement for research, these proposals will reinforce the position of our leading institutions so that they can continue to compete on the world stage; they will lay the foundations for greater collaboration between universities in the interests of all; and they will encourage research departments which are improving and well managed to raise their sights still further. This provides the basis for this country to remain a world leader.

Resources to support our strategy (£m)

	02–03	03–04	04–05	05–06	per cent Increase in cash terms in 05–06 over 02–03
DfES recurrent	990	1,071	1,098	1,237	25
OST recurrent*	664	709	767	943	42
DfES capital	153	158	208	208	36
OST capital*	103	206	245	245	138
Total	1,910	2,144	2,318	2,633	38

* Estimates of the amount of the Office of Science and Technology's UK wide funding that is likely to go to HE institutions in England. These estimates are forward projections based on spending in previous years by OST and the OST Research Councils.

Chapter 3
Higher education and business – exchanging and developing knowledge and skills

Reform

In a knowledge-based economy both our economic competitiveness and improvements in our quality of life depend on the effectiveness of knowledge sharing between business and higher education. Good business links should also play a part in tackling the low skills levels that hold back national productivity. Much has been done through specific schemes and the Higher Education Innovation Fund to improve these links. As a result, they are already excellent in some places, but good links are neither extensive nor consistent enough. To improve, institutions should increasingly be embedded in their regional economies, and closely linked with the emerging agendas of Regional Development Agencies. The nature of the role will depend upon each institution's mission and skills: for some it will be mainly national, for some closer to home. But in all cases, universities and colleges are key drivers for their regions, both economically and in terms of the social and cultural contribution they make to their communities.

Key Points and Proposals

- As announced in the Science and Innovation White Paper, the Higher Education Innovation Fund will draw together support for reach out from HE to business and become a permanent third stream of funding worth £90 million a year in 2005–06.

- Stronger partnerships will be encouraged between HE institutions in each region and the RDA and other agencies charged with promoting economic development. This will include RDAs being given a stronger role in steering the Higher Education Innovation Fund.

- There will be additional funding within the HEIF programme to set up a network of up to 20 Knowledge Exchanges to promote the critical role of less research-intensive HE institutions in transferring technologies and knowledge, and in skills development, within local communities of practice.

- We will drive forward foundation degrees, making them the main work-focused higher education qualification.

- The new sector skills councils will develop stronger alliances between business in their sectors and the relevant departments in higher education institutions both to develop and market courses and involve employers in the delivery of learning.

- We will continue to support higher education institutions in their role as community leaders, celebrating the cultural and social contribution that they make.

- We will continue to work through the TTA, the Department of Health and others as vital partners in our plans to develop the public sector workforce.

- We look forward to the findings of the Lambert Review of links between higher education and business, and the DTI/Treasury Innovation Review, and will build on our proposals in the light of them.

Introduction

3.1   Knowledge and skill transfer between business and higher education is of great importance in England's regional economies. Universities have a role in fostering the establishment and growth of new companies; in working with existing companies both on the application of the latest technology and the successful application of more tried and tested technologies; and in working with business to develop the skills of the workforce at technical and professional levels. At their best, these links should be highly interactive, with each partner well aware of what the other can offer, and of what their needs are.

3.2   The Government's strategy for science, engineering and technology, 'Investing in Innovation', set out what has been achieved so far in encouraging industry to build on publicly funded research, and to encourage links between higher education institutions and businesses. There has been considerable success, with sharp increases recently in the number of spin-off companies created, patents filed, and the proportion of universities employing specialised staff to support commercial work. Moreover, in 1999–2000 the UK created more spin-off companies per £ million of research expenditure in universities than the USA.

3.3   Much of our current performance is based on knowledge transfer from cutting-edge, internationally competitive research. This is important. But we must also make sure that businesses can access all the rest of the knowledge and expertise held by the HE sector. At the same time, we want to provide incentives for the less research intensive universities to make close and productive links with business to promote the local and regional economy.

Knowledge transfer

3.4   This is why the Government is increasing the size of the Higher Education Innovation Fund (HEIF) from 2004–05 – with £80 million available in 2004–05, and £90 million in 2005–06 – and at the same time rationalising the different schemes (including Science Enterprise Centres and University Challenge) to promote knowledge transfer and innovation. Box D gives an example of the kind of project supported by HEIF. As set out in 'Investing in Innovation', this round of HEIF will broaden the reach of knowledge transfer activities by supporting non research-intensive university departments in developing both knowledge transfer and skills development, and in reaching out not only to business but also to the regional and local economy, and the wider community. We wish to engage regional development agencies (RDAs) more closely in the distribution of HEIF funding, to make sure that it is properly focused on regional development priorities. From 2004–05, RDAs will have a larger formal role in how HEIF is distributed. HEIF will be a permanent third stream of funding for higher education institutions alongside funds for teaching and research. It will complement the Research and Development tax credits, which support businesses in investing in research and development.

3.5   As we decide how to allocate HEIF we wish to promote a clear and crucially important mission in knowledge transfer for the less research-intensive universities. We wish to see these universities concentrating on acquired technology and working mainly with local companies through consultancy rather than licensing new technology. We see staff in these institutions acquiring a group of leading edge technologies and exploiting them by creating innovative solutions to real world problems and needs, rather than themselves making breakthroughs in science or technology. To do this, they will need to link with industry in 'communities of practice' as part of their day to day teaching and research. This should provide more routes to reach small and medium-sized enterprises (SMEs) and less technologically sophisticated businesses.

BOX D: CREATIVE SERVICES INCUBATOR AT LEEDS METROPOLITAN UNIVERSITY

Leeds Metropolitan University (LMU) is using its Higher Education Innovation Fund grant to establish a business incubator with a particular focus on supporting start up companies in the creative services – such as animation, graphic design, architecture and ICT.

The incubator has been established specifically for LMU students and staff but its services will also be available to start up businesses outside the university. Businesses using the incubator will have access to specialist consultants from within the university. The initial aim is to support 100 businesses within the first three years.

Knowledge Exchanges

3.6   This new role in knowledge transfer for less research-intensive institutions is relatively under-developed in many of them. To support the strong development of this work in more areas, we want to identify best practice, and share it across the sector. The best arrangements for working with business – with support for skills development alongside provision of technology and knowledge – build a two-way process of higher education institutions and business learning about one another's needs and capabilities. Some institutions have strengths in knowledge transfer, but are less responsive to business needs for skill development; others are strong in providing work-focused programmes that respond to employer needs, but do not support business in transferring innovation.

3.7   We propose therefore to make available additional funding as a new strand of HEIF, to create a network of around 20 Knowledge Exchanges, which will be exemplars of good practice in interactions between less research-intensive institutions and business and underline the distinctive mission of these. Each Knowledge Exchange will receive up to £500,000 for each of five years. Proposals will be invited from individual institutions or institutions working in consortia with other higher education institutions or local further education colleges. To be funded, a Knowledge Exchange will need to demonstrate:

- excellent work in, or proposals for, both knowledge transfer and skill development, with relationships with employers and businesses in both the public and private sectors;

- that the funding will lead to substantial improvement in what the institution or consortium can achieve;

- strong support from employers and good partnerships with key stakeholders, including the relevant RDA, and Sector Skills Councils, and a demonstration of how its work fits into the RDA strategy, and helps serve the local and regional economy; and

- a capacity and willingness to work with other universities and colleges to spread good practice and help improve their performance.

3.8   Knowledge Exchanges will be skilled in meeting business needs, and will be able both to serve needs from within their own consortium, and to signpost businesses to other Higher Education institutions which may better meet a particular need (Box E below provides an example of the kind of work we expect Knowledge Exchanges to undertake). Eight will be open for business in 2004–05.

3.9 The Knowledge Exchanges will form part of a wider network with the New Technology Institutes that were announced in the Government's 2001 White Paper on enterprise, skills and innovation – two institutes in each region of the country based on partnerships between higher education, further education, and private sector organisations, which provide specialist ICT and other high tech learning programmes, and work closely with local companies to ensure they have the know-how to use advanced technology. Knowledge Exchanges will also be well-placed to pick up any recommendations from the Lambert and Innovation reviews.

BOX E: THE LONDON HIGHER EDUCATION CONSORTIUM (LHEC)

The LHEC provides a strategic forum for London's 40 higher education institutions and 52 further education colleges. The central purposes of the consortium are to enhance London's national and international reputation as a place for study and research, and develop the city's competitiveness and innovation. To achieve these goals, the LHEC champions collaboration between educational institutions and businesses. It supports academic research and contract work for business, and encourages senior business managers to serve on institutional governing bodies and to provide inputs into course design and development. Having gained HEFCE funding to support these initiatives, the LHEC set-up the London Competitive Advantage Programme in 2000. Specific projects have included recruiting business practitioners for teaching roles and securing work placements for students.

Strengthening the Regional Partnership

3.10 The involvement of universities and colleges in regional, social and economic development is critical. Their work in knowledge and skills transfer is not their only contribution. Institutions are significant employers in local and regional economies. In addition they have a key leadership role, are often engaged in community capacity building and regeneration and make an important contribution to civil society. Higher education's contribution to regional development very much depends on forging partnerships between institutions in each region and the RDA – as well as with other partners involved in regional skills, business, and economic development, such as the local Learning and Skills Council.

3.11 across the country, these partnerships are already growing. the higher education sector is actively engaged, along with other key partners, in the development of Regional Economic Strategies and has an important role to play in taking forward the new Frameworks for Regional Employment and Skills Action. It also has a key part to play in working with RDAs to identify the sort of business clusters that need to be fostered in their area. The RDAs are collaborating closely with universities on specific development and technology projects. They are also drawing on their new financial flexibilities to increase expenditure on knowledge transfer and innovation projects in which higher education institutions are in the lead or are key partners, and are helping to fund development of foundation degrees and other skills programmes.

3.12 The Government welcomes the moves that RDAs have made to build on the contribution of higher education to regional economies and is keen to support the strengthening of HE-RDA partnerships. We propose, in addition to RDAs playing a growing role in HEIF and other knowledge transfer programmes:

- an enhanced role for the RDAs in matching supply and demand for higher education. RDAs already have a direct input into determining new higher education provision in their regions to ensure it meets regional priorities;

- to involve RDAs further in the AimHigher campaign, to help address regional needs for access to higher education;

- to encourage RDAs to play a proactive role in developing the work of the New Technology Institutes (NTIs), including through funding; and

- to ask RDAs to take responsibility for galvanising the business community to work harder to make best use of the opportunities offered by higher education; and to play a particular role in helping small and medium-sized enterprises articulate their needs, and make links with higher education.

Higher Education and the Local Economy and Community

3.13 Higher education has a critical role to play in the community, both as a social and cultural centre and as a community leader. In some cases, universities and colleges working to serve a region together can make a dramatic impact on their community. For example, Sheffield has a 'City Strategy' in which its two universities, the University of Sheffield and Sheffield Hallam, are key partners. They have been involved in strategies to raise attainment levels throughout the FE city, as well as in a major project to enhance the city's standing as a leading location for new businesses 'spun out' from research. And institutions often have roles focused on particular sections of their community – for example, music and arts colleges support the cultural life of their communities; education faculties support schools; faculties of health and medicine play a key role in local health services; and departments of social work support local social services. We want to support institutions in developing and building on their community roles, and welcome suggestions on ways in which government can support this aspect of their work better.

Higher Education and development of skills for the workplace

DEVELOPMENT OF TECHNICAL SKILLS

3.14 The relationship between knowledge transfer and the development of technical skills in the workforce, is one of interdependence: the development of new skills can also lead to a more intelligent demand for knowledge transfer and stimulate the further development of the knowledge pool. Good higher education business links should play a part in tackling the problem of low skills that holds back our national productivity.

3.15 Higher education already makes a huge contribution to the development of the higher level technical skills that are so vital. Many of the newer universities have a strong vocational focus and have led the way in developing new courses aimed at supplying students with the skills and knowledge they need for jobs in the new, expanding areas of the economy. Growth in these subjects has been substantial. Between 1995 and 1998, the number of students graduating in design studies grew overall by 32 per cent, and in computer studies by 21 per cent. Across the higher education sector, many universities are building key employability skills into courses, as well as providing short courses to help with the continuous professional development of people already in the workforce who need to keep up with the latest changes in their field.

SECTOR SKILLS COUNCILS

3.16 Establishing close relationships between employers in particular industrial sectors and the relevant faculties in institutions is critical to preparing new entrants to the workforce and to continuous professional development. Working with the devolved administrations, we will ensure that the Sector Skills Development Agency and sector skills councils are able to work directly with the new unified teaching quality enhancement body (see Chapter 4) so that higher education has up to date knowledge of employer needs in each vocational area. sector skills councils also have a key role in bringing together universities and employers, and in helping employers to act as intelligent customers of universities so that courses that have the needs of employers at heart are developed and successfully marketed.

3.17 Sector skills councils will also engage employers with institutions on curriculum development, placements for students in industry, and exchange of staff. To support the work of sector skills councils, it will be important for universities to adopt a more strategic approach to the design and assessment of courses, and also of work experience placements, which will become ever more important as vocational provision expands. Some institutions have already made excellent progress here – for instance, over half (55 per cent) of all first-degree and diploma students at the University of Brighton undertake formal work experience placements as part of their courses.

FOUNDATION DEGREES

3.18 New two-year foundation degrees are developing well as employer-focused higher education qualifications. One of their key features is that employers play a role in designing courses, so both they and the students can be certain that they will be gaining the skills that are really needed in work (see Box F below).

3.19 Major employers like KLM and Rover have developed foundation degrees designed to meet their needs, as they modernise their workforce. And in the public sector, both the Ministry of Defence and Department of Health have found the work based approach of foundation degrees valuable. Recently, the Department of Health announced that any health service employee with 5 years service will be entitled to training and development leading to an appropriate foundation degree. For teachers, new foundation degrees are being developed as routes into some BEd courses, and dedicated foundation degrees will be part of the new standards and qualifications framework proposed for higher level teaching assistants. By providing an important route to further career development, foundation degrees have a key role to play in modernising both private and public sector workforces.

BOX F: AIRCRAFT ENGINEERING FOUNDATION DEGREE AT KINGSTON UNIVERSITY CONSORTIUM

KLM UK Engineering is a large employer of engineers in the UK. Joining forces with Kingston University Consortium it has been working to develop a foundation degree in aircraft engineering. Students have access to KLM facilities for "hands on" experience as part of their course.

Ray Flower, Chief Instructor at KLM UK Engineering says "This new qualification has been specifically designed so that it provides not only the required academic standards but also the vocational and practical experience that the industry seeks. As an active partner from the outset we've been involved in the course design. As such we've been able to ensure the course meets the needs of the industry, whilst adhering to the Joint Aviation Authority (JAA) license requirements. In addition students will be mentored and tutored by experienced engineering supervisors in operational environments."

3.20 We now need to embed foundation degrees and ensure that they are widely accepted and valued both by employers and students. As they become the major vehicle for expansion in higher education overall they will help to radically improve the delivery of technical skills to industry, business and services, not only for young people, but also for adults returning to training to update their technical skills.

3.21 To achieve this aim we propose to:

- Make foundation degrees the standard two-year qualification by enabling HNCs and HNDs to be incorporated in the foundation degree framework.

- Provide development funding to key employment sectors, HEIs and FECs to help them design new foundation degrees, so they can extend their coverage.

- Ask HEFCE to review funding levels to make sure they adequately reflect the relative costs of delivering foundation degrees compared with other forms of higher education.

- Recognise that foundation degrees are ends in their own right, giving them enhanced status as qualifications. Those with foundation degrees will have the right to use the letters 'FDA' (for arts based subjects) or 'FDSc' (for science based subjects) after their names.

- At the same time, it is important that foundation degrees form part of a coherent ladder of progression, which gives students choice about their next steps. We have decided to allow universities greater flexibility locally in determining the arrangements for progression to an honours degree, to meet the needs of students and employers.

- As we describe in Chapter 5, we will support the foundation degree route with a new national network, which will underwrite the quality of foundation degrees in FE Colleges and support their development across the board.

3.22 We also intend to encourage institutions to offer and students to take foundation degrees, and respond to economic needs by seeing more of the expansion in higher education come through this route in future years. We outline these proposals in more detail in Chapter 5.

Graduate Skills

3.23 As well as improving vocational skills, we need to ensure that all graduates, including those who study traditional academic disciplines, have the right skills to equip them for a lifetime in a fast changing work environment. Therefore, we will continue to sponsor work already under way by HEFCE to integrate the skills and attributes which employers need, such as communication, enterprise and working with others, into higher education courses, on a subject-by-subject basis.

Developing the public sector workforce

3.24 As well as providing skilled graduates to business, universities have a critical role in developing the public sector workforce. Without a strong higher education input, our hospitals, schools, and other public services would be impoverished. And as we modernise the public sector labour force, with better-developed programmes for graduate police officers and social workers, and more training for health professionals through the NHSU (a 'corporate university' for the NHS, which will be one of the world's largest learning organisations), the importance of higher education for the public services can only increase. In fact, we need around 10 per cent of graduates, and 40 per cent of maths graduates, to go into teaching alone if we are to meet our target of having 10,000 more teachers in England by 2005.

3.25 Organisations such as the Teacher Training Agency and the Department of Health play an important role, and their continued work alongside higher education institutions will be central to the modernisation of the public sector workforce. It is of vital national importance that all universities, including the leading research universities, continue to regard training for the public services – particularly the training of teachers and health professionals – as a core part of their mission.

The Lambert Review of links between higher education and business

3.26 In November 2002, the Chancellor announced a review of the way in which the higher education sector works with business, led by Richard Lambert. The review will look at ways in which collaboration between universities and business to improve innovation can be enhanced, will report by summer 2003, and will feed into the DTI Review on Innovation.

3.27 The findings of this review will represent the next major step the Government takes towards finding the most effective way to enhance the relationship between business and higher education for the good of our workforce and economy. The measures outlined in this chapter are intended as building blocks, helping institutions and businesses become closer together and work to enhance local, regional and national economies. We look forward to this work being taken forward further in the light of the findings from the Lambert review.

Resources to support our strategy (£m)

	02–03	03–04	04–05	05–06	per cent Increase in cash terms in 05–06 over 02–03
Knowledge exchanges	0		6	10	
HEIF from HEFCE	20	20	20	20	0
HEIF and other knowledge transfer from OST	42	62	75	84	100
Total	62	82	101	114	84

*   Estimates of the share of other OST knowledge transfer funding that is likely to go to HE institutions in Engand. Funding for Science Enterprise Challenge and University Challenge transfers to HEIF from 2004–05.

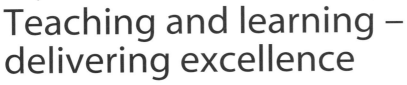

Chapter 4
Teaching and learning – delivering excellence

Reform

Teaching and learning are central to the purpose of higher education. We are committed to understanding better where and how good teaching and learning take place and to take steps to ensure that standards are high and continually improved, and that best practice is effectively shared. All students are entitled to high quality teaching, and to the best possible information to help them make the right choices about what to study and where. And those who teach well are entitled to have their success rewarded properly.

Key points and proposals

- We are rebalancing funding so that new resources come into the sector not only through research and student numbers, but through strength in teaching.

- Student choice will increasingly work to drive up quality, supported by much better information. A comprehensive survey of student views, as well as published external examiners reports and other information about teaching standards, will be pulled together in an easy-to-use Guide to Universities, overseen by the National Union of Students.

- To underpin reform, we will support improvements in teaching quality in all institutions. Additional money for pay will be conditional on higher education institutions having human resource strategies that explicitly value teaching and reward and promote good teachers.

- New national professional standards for teaching in higher education will be established as the basis of accredited training for all staff, and all new teaching staff will receive accredited training by 2006.

- The external examining system will be strengthened by improved training and induction, including a national programme for external examiners by 2004–05.

- We will also celebrate and reward teaching excellence. We are consulting on the establishment of a single national body – a teaching quality academy – which could be established by 2004 to develop and promote best practice in teaching.

- Centres of Excellence in teaching will be established to reward good teaching at departmental level and to promote best practice, with each Centre getting £500,000 a year for five years, and the chance to bid for capital funding.

- The National Teaching Fellowships Scheme will be increased in size to offer substantial rewards to twice as many outstanding teachers as at present.

- To recognise excellent teaching as a university mission in its own right, University title will be made dependent on teaching degree awarding powers – from 2004–05 it will no longer be necessary to have research degree awarding powers to become a university.

Introduction

4.1 All students are entitled to be taught well, and to be given the support they need to learn effectively. And in an era when students are being asked to contribute more to the costs of their tuition, to reflect the benefits it brings them, their expectations of teaching quality will rise. The Government believes that student choice will be an increasingly important driver of teaching quality, as students choose the good-quality courses that will bring them respected and valuable qualifications and give them the higher-level skills that they will need during their working life. But student choice can only drive quality up successfully if it is underpinned by robust information – otherwise reputations will be built on perception rather than reality. And it must also be supported by clear expectations about the standards that every university must meet, so that no student has to put up with poor teaching. There must also be clear and visible rewards for the best, to spread good practice in the system, as well as sending important signals both to students and to institutions about the value of teaching in its own right.

Providing Information for Students' Choices

INFORMATION

4.2 To become intelligent customers of an increasingly diverse provision, and to meet their own increasing diverse needs, students need accessible information. We will ensure that the views of students themselves are published in a national annual survey available for the first time in Autumn 2003, which will explicitly cover teaching quality. We also expect institutions to make progress on their own internal systems for securing student feedback.

4.3 Students decide which HEIs to apply to, and employers decide which to recruit from, based on a wide range of different factors. Students take account of information from family, friends, and careers advisers, and not just about the academic aspects of different institutions and courses. Choices are bound to be complex; but we believe that the quality of the institution's teaching should be a very important consideration. Neither students nor employers should have to base their decisions on perceptions of relative prestige which may be outdated or unreliable, but should be able to draw on up to date and robust assessments of the quality of learning and teaching.

4.4   The new arrangements for quality assurance in universities – discussed below – also require universities to publish far more information than ever before about the quality of their courses. Institutions will be expected to publish summaries of external examiners' reports – which offer clear external judgements about the quality of courses and the standards of students' work – from 2004.

4.5   But this needs to be drawn together in a helpful and clear form that students can use easily to make decisions. So we have agreed with the National Union of Students that they will take the lead in publishing a more comprehensive and easily accessible guide to higher education, that covers not only course data but other key factors such as whether the provider is a centre of excellence, the quality of its IT provision and other facilities, entry requirements, results, and the employment record of its graduates. We will make it available in user-friendly formats, with clear charts and explanations to help students compare courses, and find the best one for them.

4.6   We believe that bringing together this information, with the NUS in the lead to make sure that the focus is on the needs of the student, will be a very significant step forward in helping student demand drive up quality.

MEASURING AND RECORDING STUDENT ACHIEVEMENT

4.7   We must also ensure that we have robust ways of describing, measuring and recording student achievement which are helpful to the student, to institutions, to employers, and to other stakeholders. Existing arrangements need to be strengthened in a number of ways.

4.8   First, we will review with Universities UK, the Standing Conference of Principals, and the Quality Assurance Agency the progress being made on the use of transcripts and personal development portfolios. We want them to be used to enable learners to understand and reflect on their achievements, and to present those achievements to employers, institutions, and other stakeholders.

4.9   Second, we have asked HEFCE to review current methodologies for recording student achievement and to develop more sophisticated ways of measuring 'value added' – the distance travelled by the individual learner.

4.10 Finally, we have asked HEFCE to evaluate recent research on the honours classification system, particularly given the increasing numbers of first and upper-second class degrees being awarded. We will ask them to convene a review group with the sector to consider possible alternative methods for presenting the overall achievement of students (in addition to detailed achievements by module, subject, or individual learning experience contained on transcripts). We want to ensure that whatever system universities use is transparent and adequately conveys the difference between the achievements of individual students, so that it has credibility with students and employers. We will need to ensure that any change in methodology does not undermine the current high standing of our honours degree.

REDRESS FOR STUDENT COMPLAINTS

4.11 Reforms to give students a greater voice must include providing them with a fair, open, and transparent means of redress when things go wrong, a safeguard that will be especially important in a freer system. Last Autumn, the sector was consulted on the establishment of an independent review of student complaints. The consultation revealed that there was substantial support from HEIs for an independent adjudicator to hear student complaints, and recognition that ultimately legislation would be needed to underpin whatever arrangements were put in place.

4.12 We will, therefore, legislate for the establishment of an independent adjudicator in the forthcoming higher education bill, but have asked the sector to press ahead with establishing a voluntary independent adjudicator in the meantime. The aim is for the office of the independent adjudicator to be in place by June 2003 and ready to receive representations and adjudicate from September 2003.

Ensuring universal good provision

4.13 All students have the right to good teaching, and some may not be able to exercise their choices as easily as others – perhaps because they want to study a very specialised course, or because they would prefer to live at home. So as well as making sure that students can make well-informed choices, we must seek to guarantee good-quality teaching for everyone. This means being clearer about the teaching and learning practices and standards that students and government, as the principal funders, have a right to expect from all higher education providers. All providers should set down their expectations of teachers with reference to national professional standards; should ensure that staff are trained to teach and continue to develop professionally; should have effective quality assurance systems and robust degree standards; and should value teaching and reward good teachers.

PROFESSIONAL STANDARDS AND STAFF DEVELOPMENT

4.14 At present, there are no nationally recognised professional standards for teachers in higher education; and many of those who teach have never received any training in how to do so. In order that teaching in higher education is treated seriously as a profession in its own right, and that teachers are given the skills they need, we expect that national professional standards will be agreed by 2004–05, through the proposed new teaching quality academy, described below. These standards, to be designed and agreed by the sector itself, would then describe competences required for all teaching staff. Training of new staff to meet the standards should be possible through a wide range of different programmes and courses, as best suited to the institution and individual concerned. Once the standards are in place and command confidence across the sector we will expect all new teaching staff to obtain a teaching qualification which meets the standards from 2006. We also expect that institutions will develop policies and systems to ensure that all staff are engaged in continuing professional development to maintain, develop and update their skills.

QUALITY ASSURANCE

4.15 The QAA has performed an important role in assuring academic quality and standards in higher education. Through its assessment of teaching in Subject Reviews, it has been instrumental in defining standards for teaching, and enabling poor provision to be identified and eliminated. Recently, the QAA external review processes were radically changed to reduce the burden on higher education institutions, recognising the progress that has been made. The new model firmly places the responsibilities on institutions themselves to have robust internal systems for assuring quality and standards systems. These will be audited by independent external reviewers. More stringent and detailed external scrutiny will be reserved for problem areas – in accordance with the principle of intervention in inverse proportion to success. Achievement of satisfactory outcomes from QAA review systems will be expected of all institutions in receipt of block teaching grant. And institutions will be required to publish information about their quality and standards, as part of the reformed QAA process, to inform student choice better.

DEGREE STANDARDS

4.16 External examiners carry out a critical role in advising institutions on the comparability of their standards, and in many respects act as guardians of the public purse and of the reputation of UK higher education. As we have outlined above, a key piece of information will be available through the publication of summaries of the judgements of external examiners, giving students, parents and employers access to independent views about the standards achieved on individual courses. If these reports are to be of the highest possible standard, we need to ensure that external examiners are appropriately trained and supported, by making improvements on three fronts:

- first, by strengthening the training given by institutions, both to enable staff to fulfil their roles as internal examiners, and to prepare them to take on the role of external examining;

- second, by ensuring that institutions consistently provide full briefing and induction to their newly appointed external examiners; and

- finally, by the sector establishing a national development programme for external examiners. We look to HEFCE to take the lead in ensuring these improvements are in place by 2004–05.

REWARDING TEACHERS FOR GOOD TEACHING

4.17 In the past, rewards in higher education – particularly promotion – have been linked much more closely to research than to teaching. Indeed, teaching has been seen by some as an extra source of income to support the main business of research, rather than recognised as a valuable and high-status career in its own right. This is a situation that cannot continue. Institutions must properly reward their best teaching staff; and all those who teach must take their task seriously.

4.18 We know from HEFCE's Rewarding and Developing Staff in Higher Education initiative that institutions are taking positive steps to create and retain a flexible, motivated and continually improving cadre of teachers and other staff who support learning. The Learning and Teaching Committee National Co-ordination Team has been able to draw on a number of examples of excellent work in institutions for its good practice guide on 'Recognising and Rewarding Excellent Teaching' (The Open University, 2002 – see box G).

> **BOX G: EXTRACT FROM 'RECOGNISING AND REWARDING EXCELLENT TEACHING'**
>
> The learning and teaching strategy of the University of Central Lancashire sets out "to develop a culture in which excellence in developing learning is recognised and rewarded at individual and team levels … the University will, as a priority, raise the status, recognition and rewards for the learning and teaching role of staff to a level equivalent to that given to research". Its learning and teaching strategy explicitly addresses the existing culture and sets out to change it, using the Human Resource Strategy to help achieve this.
>
> The University has included learning and teaching criteria for the first time in its Academic Promotions Scheme to recognise and reward exceptional achievement by individual members of staff. Eleven such appointments to Principal Lecturer were made in the first year of operation of the strategy.

4.19 But good practice must become universal. All institutions need to develop strategies and systems for recruitment, performance management, training and career development which explicitly value teaching and reward and promote individual teachers. Critical to this will be strategies for pay.

Fair pay in higher education

4.20 If university managers are to deliver the high quality we expect from higher education, it is essential that institutions are able to recruit and then retain staff of the highest calibre. The recent annual HEFCE survey provided evidence of a worrying rise in unfilled vacancies across the university workforce. Among academics, particular recruitment difficulties were reported in a range of subjects (IT/computing, business-related subjects, professions allied to medicine, science, and engineering) where higher salaries were on offer elsewhere.[23] At the same time, as reported in the recent Roberts review, there are anecdotal reports of a decline in the quality of new applicants for academic jobs.[24]

4.21 The Government invested £50 million in 2001–02, £110 million in 2002–03 and has planned for £170 million for 2003–04 to underpin the recruitment, retention and reward plans set out in HEIs' human resources strategies. HEFCE has distributed this money to institutions in return for human resource strategies that address issues of recruitment and retention, staff and management development, equal opportunities, rewarding good performance and tackling poor performance. This process has successfully kick-started the modernisation of human resource management in higher education, allowing institutions to play to their strengths and reward excellence.

4.22 Over the coming period, the Government will pursue a twin-track strategy for academic pay. Firstly, it will build on the progress achieved through this funding for institutional-level human resources plans. In addition to that funding, the government is providing an extra £50 million in 2004–05 and £117 million in 2005–06. We want to remove the bureaucracy of the ring-fence, and give higher education institutions the freedom to spend this money as they see fit, but we also want to sustain the cultural change that the human resource strategies have begun. So, once individual institutions have human resource strategies that demonstrate to HEFCE that they will take steps to move towards market supplements or other differentiated means of recruiting and retaining staff, and commit themselves to rewarding good performance, their earmarked funding will be transferred into block teaching grant.

4.23 Secondly, we are especially keen to see better pay differentiation for teachers, with institutions rewarding those who teach well. Therefore, from the additional funding for

23 Recruitment and retention of staff in UK higher education 2001.
24 SET for success, The supply of people with science, technology, engineering and mathematics skills, The report of the Sir Gareth Roberts Review, April 2002, esp. 5.34–5.

teaching excellence which we have identified over the next three years, we will ask HEFCE to release funds to those institutions that can demonstrate that it will be spent on rewards for their best teaching staff.

Spreading Best Practice in Teaching

4.24 We need to foster an environment of continuous improvement in the development of learning and teaching in institutions. Substantial investment has been made through the national Teaching Quality Enhancement Fund – over £180 million between 1999 and 2005. But it is widely acknowledged that work on the development and dissemination of good practice at the national level is fragmented.

4.25 The final report of the joint HEFCE/UUK/SCOP group, the 'Teaching Quality Enhancement Committee' addresses these issues and recommends the creation of a new unitary body (referred to in this document as a 'teaching quality academy'). We welcome the work of the committee as an important contribution to raising the status of teaching in higher education. The new organisation that it proposes would bring together the functions of the Institute for Learning and Teaching in Higher Education (ILTHE), the Learning and Teaching Support Network (LTSN), and the Higher Education Staff Development Agency (HESDA). Its overarching role would be to support continuous professional development for teaching in HE, by sponsoring and developing good practice, setting professional standards, accrediting training, conducting research, and helping develop policy on teaching and learning. It would work closely with the emerging sector skills council, which will be led by employers with responsibility for skills in higher education and the wider adult learning sector across the UK.

Rewards for Excellence

4.26 As well as having their good practice spread to others, it is right that those who teach outstandingly well should be rewarded. Their excellence should also be celebrated and made visible, which will both help students make choices and help drive cultural change in the value attached to good teaching in higher education.

INDIVIDUAL REWARDS FOR EXCELLENCE

4.27 More needs to be done to highlight and reward truly outstanding individual teachers as role models for the rest of the profession. The National Teaching Fellowship Scheme has been highly successful, offering prizes of £50,000 to 20 outstanding teachers and we will therefore expand the scheme over time to provide over twice as many fellowships – up to 50.

4.28 We should also celebrate excellent practice in teaching departments. The very best will be designated as Centres of Excellence, and given funding of £500,000 a year for five years to reward academics and to fund extra staff to help promote and spread their good pedagogical practice. These Centres will be identified through a process of peer review managed by HEFCE and drawing wherever possible on existing information.[25] Their status will help to raise the profile of excellent teaching, as well as helping them to attract students. 70 Centres will be identified by 2006 and, depending on successful evaluation of the programme, we hope to expand it in the future.

4.29 In order to recognise the good work of those departments that come close to, but do not quite meet, the standard to become a Centre of Excellence, HEFCE will also offer a 'commended' status. This will recognise those departments' achievement, and make it clear to prospective students that they can expect a particularly high standard of teaching on their courses.

4.30 Centres of Excellence will be able to bid for capital funding of up to £2m each, for improving their teaching infrastructure and estates. Capital funding for teaching will help to make sure that the learning environment and equipment gives a better experience to students, keeps pace with the skill of the lecturers, and plays its part in raising the status of learning at an institutional level.

University Title – focusing on teaching

4.31 At present, the 'University' title is reserved for institutions that have the power to award both taught degrees, and research degrees. The right to award research degrees requires that the institution demonstrate its strength in research. This situation is at odds with our belief that institutions should play to diverse strengths, and that excellent teaching is, in itself, a core mission for a university (see Box H overleaf). It is clear that good scholarship, in the sense of remaining aware of the latest research and thinking within a subject, is essential for good teaching, but not that it is necessary to be active in cutting-edge research to be an excellent teacher.

4.32 This is borne out by a number of studies undertaken over the last ten years. A report in the mid 90s looked at 58 studies which contained ratings of both research and teaching, and found no relationship between the two.[26] More recently, a report to HEFCE in 2000, involving contributions from more than 40 universities and colleges, concluded that not every teacher needs to be engaged in 'research' as a narrowly defined activity but might be expected to

---

25 These departments (or other similarly-sized teaching units) might be in any institution delivering higher education, including Higher Education Colleges, mixed economy FE colleges, or initial teacher training or health professions providers.

26 *The Relationship Between Research and Teaching. A Meta-Analysis;* Hattie and March Review of Educational Research (1996).

engage in scholarship to inform their work as teachers.[27] These findings are backed up by the experience of our current colleges of higher education. These higher education colleges have standards of teaching that, in many cases, match or even surpass those of full universities.

BOX H: THE CALIFORNIA STATE UNIVERSITY (CSU) SYSTEM

The CSU is America's largest four-year university system with 23 campuses located throughout the state of California. Its primary mission is to be a teaching-centred comprehensive university, rather than be research-based. Offering professional training to those students who wish to be teachers, nurses, social workers and engineers (for example), CSU is open to freshmen who are placed in the top third of California high school graduates.

Proving that it is not necessary for popular universities to be primarily research-based, enrolment in CSU is rising: total enrolment in the 2002–03 academic year stands at 400,000 students. Projection is for an increase of 100,000 full-time-equivalent students by 2010. The Accrediting Commission of the Western Association of Schools and Colleges (WASC) singled out one of the larger campuses of the university as being of "exceptional quality".

4.33 We propose to change the system, so that the University title is awarded on the basis of taught degree awarding powers, student numbers, and the range of subjects offered. This will send an important signal about the importance of teaching, and about the benefits for some institutions of focusing their efforts on teaching well.

4.34 At the same time, we will examine and modernise the criteria for degree-awarding powers to reflect the increasing diversity of higher education. The current system does not sufficiently reflect factors such as new virtual learning models, or the legitimate roles of those outside the university sector in providing high quality higher education learning. But there will be no relaxation of the high standards that have to be reached before taught degree awarding powers are granted.

4.35 These changes to the criteria for degree awarding powers and University title will be taken forward via a review which we will commission from the QAA, consulting widely within England and with the devolved administrations, and introducing new legislation as necessary. We expect changes to come into force during 2004–05.

---

27 *Interactions between Research, Teaching and Other Academic Activities:* Report to the HEFCE as part of the Fundamental Review of Research Policy and Funding (HEFCE, 2000).

Resources to support our strategy (£m)*

	02–03	03–04	04–05	05–06	per cent Increase in cash terms in 05–06 over 02–03
Recurrent, of which	3,788	4,024	4,227	4,521	19
Human Resources	110	170	220	287	
Teaching Excellence	0	5	33	71	
Capital	155	207	377	442	185
Total	3,943	4,230	4,604	4,963	26

*   Sum of columns may not match totals, owing to rounding.

Chapter 5
Expanding higher education to meet our needs

Reform

The economic case for expanding the provision of higher education is extremely strong. But as we expand, we must not compromise on quality, and we must make sure that the courses and patterns of study on offer really match the needs of our economy, and the demands of students themselves. We must not and will not pursue expansion for its own sake, simply by offering more of what has always been offered before.

Key Points and Proposals

- National economic imperatives support our target to increase participation in higher education towards 50 per cent of those aged 18–30 by the end of the decade. Participation in England is already 43 per cent.

- The bulk of the expansion will come through new types of qualification, tailored to the needs of students and of the economy. Our emphasis will be on the expansion of two-year work-focused foundation degrees, as they become the primary work-focused higher education qualification.

- We will support employers to develop more foundation degrees focusing on the skills they really need; we will encourage students to take them by offering financial incentives for them; and we will fund additional places for foundation degrees rather than traditional three-year honours degrees.

- Foundation degrees will often be delivered in Further Education colleges, and we will build and strengthen the links between further and higher education, to give students clearer progression pathways and support the development of work-based degrees. As part of this, we will streamline the funding regimes to make collaboration easier.

- We will establish 'Foundation Degree Forward', a network of Universities which are leading the development of foundation degrees, both as a catalyst for the further development, a reservoir of good practice, and to provide a validation service for foundation degrees offered in further education, so that students can be completely confident about their quality.

- We will also encourage other sorts of flexible provision, which meet the needs of an increasingly diverse student body, by improving more support for those doing part-time degrees, and supporting the development of flexible "2+" arrangements, credit transfer, and e-learning.

The Case for Expansion

ECONOMY

5.1 Society is changing. Our economy is becoming ever more knowledge-based – we are increasingly making our living through selling high-value services, rather than physical goods. These trends demand a more highly-skilled workforce. Forecasts by the Institute for Employment Research show that between 1999 and 2010 the number of jobs in higher level occupations – the ones most likely to be filled by those who have been through higher education – will grow by over one and a half million.[28] That represents 80 per cent of new jobs over the decade. Almost half of these jobs will be at the associate professional and higher technician level – best served through effective work-focused programmes.

5.2 But we know that this is not the whole picture. The economy also needs people with modern skills at all levels. We are not choosing between more plumbers and more graduates. We need both, and we need to help individuals to make sensible and appropriate choices. The Government's Skills Strategy, to be published this year, will set out our proposals for raising the skills of the workforce at all levels, and ensuring that the education and training system responds effectively to demand from employers.

5.3 A comprehensive review of the academic literature[29] suggests that there is compelling evidence that education increases productivity, and moreover that higher education is the most important phase of education for economic growth in developed countries, with increases in HE found to be positively and significantly related to per capita income growth. The review also found that education is highly likely to give rise to further indirect effects on growth, by stimulating more effective use of resources, and more physical capital investment and technology adoption.

5.4 Higher education qualifications are more than a signal to the labour market – they bring real skills benefits which employers are prepared to pay a significant premium for. The fact that studying different subjects brings different labour market benefits (which can't be explained by the qualifications the students began the course with) argues strongly that employers are responding to real and significant skills and qualities resulting from higher education qualifications.

28 Wilson, R.A., and Green, A.E, (2001). *Projections of Occupations and Qualifications 2000/01: Research in Support of the National Skills Task Force*. Sheffield: Department for Education and Employment.

29 *The Returns to Education: A Review of the Macro-Economic Literature;* Barbara Sianesi and John Van Reenen, (March 2002: Institute for Fiscal Studies Working Paper 2002/05.) – It should be noted, though, that there are both data limitations and methodological problems in isolating the contribution of any particular factor empirically.

5.5   For the individual, the economic benefits of higher education are well-documented – quite apart from the opportunity for personal and intellectual fulfilment. Graduates and those who have 'sub-degree' qualifications earn, on average, around 50 per cent more than non-graduates. Graduates are half as likely to be unemployed, and as a group they have enjoyed double the number of job promotions over the last five years, compared to non-graduates.[30] Higher education also brings social benefits – there is strong evidence that suggests that graduates are likely to be more engaged citizens. For instance, one Home Office report found a strong positive correlation between the cohesiveness of local communities and participation in higher education.[31]

5.6   Even though the number of graduates has risen significantly over the last twenty years, the gap between graduate and average earnings hasn't narrowed at all. If anything, it has increased. And the returns to HE are higher in the UK than in any other OECD country – in fact, the OECD's report describes the UK as being "in a group of its own".[32] So there are real jobs available and no reason to believe that higher education will lose its value as more young people are educated to higher levels – especially if the main part of the increase comes in new and employer-responsive types of degree.

The 50 per cent target

5.7   For all these reasons, we believe that our target to increase participation in higher education towards 50 per cent of those aged 18–30 by the end of the decade, linked to our wider aim to prepare 90 per cent of young people for higher education or skilled employment, is right. Moreover, since on latest estimates England currently has a participation rate for 18–30 year olds of 43 per cent,[33] the further increase we need to achieve 50 per cent by 2010 is relatively modest. The chart overleaf shows how other countries compare, using the nearest comparable OECD measure.

30 Taylor Nelson Sofres Omnibus Survey, 2002.

31 *Community Cohesion: A report of the independent review team chaired by Ted Cantle,* Home Office: 2001.

32 *Education at a Glance 2002*; OECD, p. 127.

33 For English-domiciled students in UK HE.

Entry rates to tertiary education (2000)[34]

Country	Net entry rate for 'Tertiary type A' (first degree or equivalent)
Finland	71 per cent
New Zealand	70 per cent
Sweden	67 per cent
Iceland	66 per cent
Poland	62 per cent
Australia	59 per cent
Norway	59 per cent
Netherlands	51 per cent
Spain	48 per cent
United Kingdom	46 per cent
Korea	45 per cent
Italy	43 per cent
United States	43 per cent
Japan	39 per cent
France	37 per cent
Germany	30 per cent
Denmark	29 per cent

5.8   But we do not believe that expansion should mean 'more of the same'. There is a danger of higher education becoming an automatic step in the chain of education – almost a third stage of compulsory schooling. We do not favour expansion on the single template of the traditional three year honours degree.

5.9   Our overriding priority is to ensure that as we expand higher education places, we ensure that the expansion is of an appropriate quality and type to meet the demands of employers and the needs of the economy and students. We believe that the economy needs more work-focused degrees – those, like our new foundation degrees, that offer specific, job-related skills.

5.10 We want to see expansion in two-year, work-focused foundation degrees; and in mature students in the workforce developing their skills. As we do this, we will maintain the quality standards required for access to university, both safeguarding the standards of traditional honours degrees and promoting a step-change in the quality and reputation of work-focused courses.

5.11 We welcome the fact that an objective review of the way in which the 50 per cent target is measured (the Initial Entry Rate) has just begun – led by the Office for National Statistics. Views are invited via the National Statistics website until the end of February 2003[35]. The aim is to increase the rigour and transparency of the method for measuring our progress.

34 OECD, Education at a Glance 2002.

35 www.statistics.gov.uk

Changing the pattern of provision

5.12 There is good evidence to suggest that the skills gap is most acute at a level that is served well by what has traditionally been termed 'sub-degree' provision – two year provision that is work-focused. The National Skills Task Force reported that jobs at the associate professional and higher technician level will experience the greatest growth in the coming years, increasing by 790,000 up to 2010. The Employer Skills Survey 2002 found that associate professional occupations were a 'hot-spot' for skills shortage vacancies.[36]

5.13 But work-focused higher education courses focused on this skill level have suffered from social and cultural prejudice against vocational education. Employers claim that they want graduates whose skills are better fitted for work; but the labour market premium they pay still favours traditional three-year honours degrees. Graduates with honours degrees earn 64 per cent more than those without degrees, but including two-year work-focused courses, the figure drops to 50 per cent. And students have therefore continued to apply for three-year honours courses in preference.

5.14 New foundation degrees are making a good start as a reputable and truly employer-focused higher education qualification. In Chapter 3, we discussed the benefits that stem from involving employers properly in the design of courses, and outlined our proposals to make foundation degrees the standard two-year higher education qualification, by working to bring HNDs and HNCs into the foundation degree framework, and by providing development funding to key employment sectors, HEIs and FECs to help them design new foundation degrees, so they can extend their coverage of different sectors of employment. We will reinforce the value and significance of foundation degrees as qualifications in their own right. Holders of foundation degrees will be able to use the letters FDA or FDSc after their name, depending on whether their foundation degrees are arts or science based.

5.15 The proposed deregulation of fees set out in Chapter 7 will give institutions the flexibility to position their programmes in accordance with the costs of and perceived returns to particular qualifications. Foundation degrees are likely to be priced competitively in such a market.

5.16 But in order to get over the barrier of unfamiliarity and suspicion with which new courses are often regarded, and catalyse a change in the pattern of provision in the sector, we also intend to incentivise both the supply of and the demand for foundation degrees.

5.17 *For institutions*, we will offer additional funded places for foundation degrees from 2004, in preference to traditional honours degree courses; so that the numbers studying traditional three-year courses will remain steady, and growth will come predominantly through this

36 *Employer Skills Survey 2002* Department for Education and Skills (2002).

important new route. We will also provide development funding for institutions and employers to work together in designing more new foundation degree courses, discussed in more detail in Chapter 3.

5.18 *For students*, we will provide incentives for those doing foundation degrees, in the form of bursaries which might be used either for extra maintenance, or to offset the fee for the course. We will provide £10 million in 2004–05, rising to £20 million in 2005–06, for these incentives.

5.19 We believe that these stimuli are necessary to break the traditional pattern of demand. Focusing more on two-year courses will serve both our economy's needs, and our young people, better in the future. But we know that we will only succeed in changing the pattern of provision if foundation degrees are valuable to employers, attractive to students, and supported by institutions. We cannot impose this change. So we welcome views on what more government can do to support the development of foundation degrees; and in particular on whether we have got the proposed incentives right.

Delivering Higher Education in Further Education

5.20 Further education colleges already play an important role in delivering higher education – they currently deliver 11 per cent of higher education. The vast majority of this (around 90 per cent) comprises two year work-focused programmes, including new foundation degrees, which means that delivery through further education will be especially important as we reshape the pattern of expansion.

5.21 Further education has strengths in providing ladders of progression for students, particularly for those pursuing vocational routes, and serves the needs of part-time students and those who want to study locally. Further education colleges make an important contribution to meeting local and regional skills needs, including through the higher education they provide. We want this significant role to continue and to grow. However, it will be important that any expanded provision is of the high quality that we expect from higher education. We believe that structured partnerships between colleges and universities – franchise or consortium arrangements with colleges funded through partner HEIs – will be the primary vehicles to meet these aims and will deliver the best benefits for learners.

5.22 However, there will be some instances – such as where 'niche' provision is delivered or where there are no obvious higher education partners – where direct funding of higher education in further education colleges may be more appropriate. These will be considered on a case by case basis by HEFCE, against criteria which will include critical mass, track record on quality and standards, and nature of provision. HEFCE will issue new guidelines on the supply of places and funding of provision through colleges.

National Body for Foundation Degrees

5.23 Many further education colleges are working effectively with partner universities which formally award the foundation degrees they offer. In the best partnerships, these universities actively support the programmes and offer a real guarantee of quality to the student. However, not all further education colleges have local universities in the position to develo egree programmes with them in such a close and supportive way. To address this and to widen the choice for further education colleges, and other colleges without degree-awarding powers, we will establish a new national network of universities – "Foundation Degree Forward" – to offer a dedicated validation service for foundation degrees. It will also act as a national centre for foundation degree expertise, liaising with sector skills councils and professional bodies to draw up frameworks for foundation degrees covering a wide range of skills needs.

FE-HE collaboration

5.24 As part of making it easier to form sensible partnerships across the further education/higher education boundary, government will remove unnecessary bureaucracy where provision crosses sectors and will provide equity for both providers and learners. We believe that there are unnecessary difficulties for collaboration between higher education and further education presented by the need to respond to the two different funding council regimes in relation to planning, funding, and data collection, as well as the difficulties of juggling the requirements of the two quality assurance and inspection arrangements. Different 'mixed economy' institutions and federal arrangements are developing where the traditional boundaries are no longer relevant or desirable. We will work with HEFCE and the LSC to take forward ways of reducing the difficulties 'mixed economy' institutions currently face as a consequence of operating within two funding regimes. This will include reviewing the administrative and legislative barriers that exist to improve greater integration of systems.

Inclusive and Flexible Teaching and Learning

5.25 As more people from non-traditional backgrounds go into higher education we must make sure that they are well-served when they get there. The application rate for mature students is continuing to rise, including applications for part-time study. Following that trend, we expect more people to study while at work, perhaps building on modern apprenticeships. So there must be more flexible ways of learning that attract people with different demands and commitments. We have described our proposals for increasing the number of foundation degree places. It is also important that opportunities for part-time and flexible study, including e-learning, continue to increase.

There are a number of ways of providing additional flexibility:

- "2+" models offer an important model for more flexible higher study, with students undertaking the first two years of a degree, or an alternative programme – perhaps a foundation degree – in one institution, and having the opportunity to move to another to complete a full honours degree, often but not always over a further one or two years. We will be working with HEFCE to develop a framework for funding and incentivising more "2+2" and "2+1" style provision to take forward the work that has already been done in the sector.

- Credit systems, which make it possible to break off and start again without having to repeat learning, will become increasingly important as the routes into and through higher education become more varied. They help motivate learners, recognising achievement along the way; and they help institutions develop flexible curricula. Many institutions have internal credit systems, and there are a number of consortia with shared ones (see Box I). HEFCE will work with partners in the sector – from 2003 onwards – to build upon the best current practice, and to scale this up so that there is widespread and consistent use of credit across higher education.

BOX I: CREDIT ACCUMULATION WITHIN THE DERBYSHIRE ACCESS NETWORK

The Derbyshire Access Network has built a partnership between the University of Derby and local FE institutions, within which a local credit system has been developed and is now recognised throughout the partnership institutions.

The system is underpinned by numerical grades reflecting academic achievement within an agreed standards framework, and has helped smooth progression from further into higher education, and given students greater control over the direction and pace of their studies, as well as helping the university and colleges to respond flexibly to the growing diversity of students' needs. During 2002, the Access Network helped over 500 students, of whom 46 per cent had no formal qualifications.

- ICT and e-learning offer another flexible way to study, and also make it easier to share teaching material within and between institutions (see Box J over). The Open University has over 160,000 students accessing online services for their courses, some 20,000 of whom are studying from overseas. HEFCE has set up the UK e-Universities project to encourage HEIs to work together and make the development of e-learning more affordable, sharing the development costs of e-learning materials to reduce the barriers to market entry. HEFCE will now work with partners on plans to embed e-learning in a full and sustainable way within the next ten years.

BOX J: ICT-BASED HIGHER EDUCATION AT THE UNIVERSITY OF COVENTRY

Coventry University runs an online learning environment, based on WebCT, which provides resources and learning management support for students in six different schools of study. Students can access a wide range of online study tools: lecture support resources, interactive quizzes, discussion areas for contact with fellow students and tutors, study calendars, assignment dates and study skill support.

■ A further possible flexible form of provision is the compressed two-year honours degree, with a different pattern of terms and shorter holidays. This may suit those who would have difficulty spending a full three years in full-time education, but who have the enthusiasm and the drive to complete a higher education degree. The Flowers report[37] considered the extension of the teaching year by using the summer as a third semester. This would allow students to complete degrees over two years, and also allow more flexible work patterns. Again, funding patterns do not currently support this sort of provision particularly well, but we will establish a pilot to encourage institutions to try out two-year honours degrees, and evaluate them carefully.

Recruiting international students

5.26 We have a very strong record in recruiting international students, and as we expand our provision we should build on this record. People who are educated in the UK promote Britain around the world, helping our trade and diplomacy, and also providing an important economic benefit. British exports of education and training are worth some eight billion pounds a year – money that feeds into our institutions and helps open up opportunities for more people to study. The Prime Minister has set us the target of attracting an extra 50,000 higher education students to the UK from outside Europe by 2005. Institutions are currently well on track to meet this, having already recruited an additional 31,000 by 2001–02 . Working closely with the British Council, we are promoting our higher education across the world, including intensive work in many countries and bringing together all of the relevant information on the internet. We are pioneering the New Route PhD courses, now offered by 31 universities in England, as fully competitive with the best in the world. And many individual universities and colleges are dedicating their own efforts to targeted recruitment.

---

37   *The Review of the Academic Year*; A report of the Committee of Enquiry into the Organisation of the Academic Year, HEFCE (1993).

Resources to support our strategy (£m)

	02–03	03–04	04–05	05–06	per cent Increase in cash terms in 05–06 over 02–03
Foundation Degree development	0	9	11	12	
Foundation Degree incentives	0	0	10	20	
Total	0	9	21	32	

* Additional funds for growth in higher education are also included in the teaching and student support chapters.

Chapter 6
Fair access

Reform

Education must be a force for opportunity and social justice, not for the entrenchment of privilege. We must make certain that the opportunities that higher education brings are available to all those who have the potential to benefit from them, regardless of their background. This is not just about preventing active discrimination; it is about working actively to make sure that potential is recognised and fostered wherever it is found.

Key Points and Proposals

- Raising participation and standards through our reforms of secondary and further education is critical to widening access.

- But we must also raise the aspirations of schools and young people. A unified national AimHigher programme will build better links between schools, colleges and universities, including through summer schools and a pilot programme offering students the chance to support teachers in schools and colleges.

- We will ensure that there are good-quality and accessible 'second-chance' routes into higher education for those who missed out when they were younger.

- And we will work with universities to make sure that admissions procedures are professional, fair and transparent, and use the widest possible range of information about students when making decisions.

- Institutions will be provided with better benchmark data on which to judge progress in widening access and we will continue to support the work being done to secure fair access to the most prestigious universities.

- We will ask HEFCE to reform the access premium so that universities and colleges will be properly funded for the extra costs of attracting and retaining students from non-traditional backgrounds.

- Universities with unacceptably high drop-out rates will be asked to plan improvements.

- We will appoint a Higher Education Access Regulator, who will develop a framework for Access Agreements for each institution. Only institutions making satisfactory progress on access will be able to participate in the Graduate Contribution Scheme from 2006.

- We will reintroduce grants for students from the lowest income families, to help overcome their financial worries and to underpin a raising of aspirations. Proposals for this are set out in Chapter 7.

Introduction

6.1   The Government's commitment to fair access will not waver. All those who have the potential to benefit from higher education should have the opportunity to do so. This is a fundamental principle which lies at the heart of building a more socially just society, because education is the best and most reliable route out of poverty and disadvantage.

6.2   There is no simple means of achieving wider access. Success in opening up higher education to all who have the potential to benefit from it depends on building aspirations and attainment throughout all stages of education. Higher education institutions need to be supported in their efforts to reach out to students from non-traditional backgrounds, and provide them with the right pastoral and teaching support; young people and their families need to be encouraged to raise their aspirations and achieve more of their potential in examinations prior to entry to higher education; and finally, there must be an effective and fair system of student support that takes into account the different circumstances of an increasingly varied student population. Student support is discussed more fully in Chapter 7.

Higher Standards in Schools and Colleges

6.3   The single most important cause of the social class division in higher education participation is differential attainment in schools and colleges. While around 43 per cent of 18 year olds from higher socio-economic backgrounds gain two or more A-levels, only 19 per cent of those from lower socio-economic backgrounds do so. Given that 9 out of 10 people with 2 or more A-levels go on to higher education by the time they are 21, this shows why our reforms to raise standards across the piece in education, beginning in early childhood and going on through schools and colleges, are so important to our higher education agenda. It is worth noting that students from lower socio-economic groups who do achieve good A-levels are as likely to go on to university as young people from better-off backgrounds.

6.4   Standards have risen dramatically in primary schools and a substantial reform programme is now taking place in secondary education. Last year saw England's best ever GCSE and A-level results. The Government's 14–19 strategy, published on January 21, will promote higher aspirations and levels of attainment by age 19. The 'Success for All' programme for further education, which focuses on raising standards of teaching and learning, will also make a vital contribution – over 40 per cent of higher education entrants come through colleges.

Raising Aspirations

6.5   Raising school standards is critical, but it will not be enough on its own. More young people must be motivated to stay on in learning after age 16 and more of those who achieve the requisite qualifications at age 18 or 19 must be encouraged to consider going on to higher education. The roll out of Education Maintenance Allowances (see Box K) across the country will encourage more young people from less well off families to stay on in learning. It is especially important that those who come from families without a tradition of going to higher education, and whose aspirations are low, are supported both in achieving their full potential before university, and in aspiring to go on to further study.

BOX K: EDUCATION MAINTENANCE ALLOWANCES

Education Maintenance Allowances (EMAs) are a 'something for something' measure. Eligible young people aged 16–19 (or their parents in a few areas) can receive an allowance of up to £30 a week (£40 a week in Oldham and Nottingham) if they stay on at school or college, and sign a learning agreement which sets out details of their course, attendance, and homework requirements. EMAs are currently being piloted in 56 Local Education Authority areas across England, and findings from the original 15 pilots show a gain in participation for young people of around 5.9 percentage points. On 15 July 2002, the Chancellor announced that the EMA pilot scheme would be extended across England from 2004, with EMAs worth up to £1,500 a year for those who stay on and study.

6.6   There are still significant barriers of aspiration facing young people from non-traditional backgrounds, as well as disabled students and those from some ethnic minority groups. 59 per cent of a sample of 16–30 year olds from social classes C1, C2, D and E did not plan ever to go to university, and almost half of the sample had never thought about doing a degree. 45 per cent of the sample agreed that 'the student image is not for me'. And aspirations are often set at an early age – one study found that the decision to participate in higher education was made by the age of 14 by the majority of pupils, and some made the decision even earlier.[38]

---

38 MORI. The figures are based on a representative sample of 16–30 year olds living in England and Wales from social classes C1, C2, D and E. These findings are confirmed by provisional baseline figures from the evaluation of Excellence Challenge which is currently underway. (UCAS, "Paving the Way", 2002).

6.7 Early experience of the Excellence Challenge programme has suggested that it is important for universities working closely with schools and colleges in disadvantaged areas to provide good information and the chance to visit and experience a 'taster' of university, to help raise aspirations. So from 2003–04 the level of support provided by the Excellence Challenge programme will be increased, and its coverage widened. We will bring the programme together with the Partnerships for Progression initiative to deliver a coherent national outreach programme to be called "AimHigher", operating most intensively in the most disadvantaged areas. Box L gives an example of the kind of work supported by Excellence Challenge.

BOX L: UNIVERSITY OF LIVERPOOL

Using funds from the Excellence Challenge and elsewhere, the University of Liverpool is working closely with schools and colleges in Merseyside to widen access. Masterclasses and residential courses have provided opportunities for about 4,000 young people to improve their attainment and get a taste of university life. In particular, the "Talent Support" programme has paired student mentors with young people with no family history of higher education who work together after school and at week-ends to dispel myths and stereotypes. As a result of all these activities, Liverpool's record on admitting students from disadvantaged backgrounds is one of the best of the Russell Group of universities.

6.8 As part of AimHigher, we will also provide funding for a pilot initiative to encourage students to undertake paid, part-time support roles in schools or colleges, building on existing work such as the 'Teacher Associate' scheme run by the TTA. Many young people lack role models who can give them a clear, first-hand view about what university life is like, and what the benefits of going to university are. Students will be able to share their experiences with the young people they work with, and in return will get paid for valuable work experience.

6.9 London has a large number of higher education institutions, and is uniquely well placed to offer opportunities for young people in its schools and colleges to understand and experience what higher education can offer. We are keen to test some innovative approaches to partnerships through workshops, mentoring, taster courses, and in some schools, close involvement with higher education staff in schools with low progression to higher education so that parents and pupils come to see higher education as a natural choice.

6.10 Another AimHigher Roadshow[39] is underway this year and will be repeated. This year it will reach 54,000 year 9 pupils and over 15,000 students in FE and sixth form colleges. The potential impact of this campaign is already becoming clear – when asked whether they were interested in, or definitely going to university, 75 per cent of attendees said 'yes' after a roadshow compared to 52 per cent beforehand.

39 Sponsored by Royal Bank of Scotland/NatWest.

6.11 Effective support mechanisms within institutions are essential to attracting and retaining vulnerable students, offering pastoral, academic and financial advice services. Many institutions have already recognised that this can be done very effectively through one stop shops, or other integrated facilities, such as the new Student Services Centre at the University of Manchester and the innovative HE 'shop in the High Street' run by the University of Wolverhampton. The Department has been encouraging all institutions to improve these services, and plans to publish in the Spring, a digest of examples of good practice by student services. It has provided earmarked funding to support and promote student finance advice.

6.12 The Department has also commissioned a study to examine the experiences of ethnic minority students, which will identify and assess the factors which affect participation, student achievement and transition into the labour market. This will report in 2004.

Other Routes and Second Chances

6.13 Of course, not all higher education entrants come straight from school or college – over half of those currently in higher education are over 25, and meeting their needs will continue to be an important function of the system in Britain and elsewhere, especially given the pressures generated by the knowledge economy and the prospect of lengthening working lives.[40] Access to higher education courses have provided a valuable entry route into higher education for many students, particularly those mature learners who missed out at 18. However, numbers have not increased significantly over the past few years. We will ask the Quality Assurance Agency for Higher Education to come forward with proposals to modernise the criteria for Access Courses so that they are sufficiently flexible and attractive to meet the needs of today's adult learners.

6.14 A key role in supporting participation among under-represented groups is played by further and higher education colleges, and by the seven long-term residential colleges (see Box M). We will develop and encourage this form of provision which continues to offer major opportunities.

> **BOX M: RUSKIN COLLEGE AND THE LONG TERM RESIDENTIAL COLLEGES**
>
> The role of long-term residential colleges was first shaped more than a century ago by Ruskin College, which developed provision for trade unionists and working class people to prepare for higher education. More recently the colleges have offered higher education provision in direct partnership with higher education institutions. Since the 1980s, this work has been paralleled for adults who cannot take up residential provision by Access course provision in further education colleges and specialist adult education provision across the country.

---

40 Note that some of these are entering higher education for a second time.

Admissions

6.15 If we succeed in raising aspirations among non-traditional students, many more of them will apply. So it will be critical that institutions are supported in ensuring that these new applicants are treated fairly, while being tested appropriately for their potential for higher education. The new Access Regulator described later in this chapter will have a key role in overseeing fair entrance to higher education, but it is not for the government to prescribe admissions systems, for which universities themselves are responsible. We look to them to ensure that their admissions criteria are as easily understood as possible, and that admissions staff, both academic and administrative, are properly trained so that they can recognise genuine potential as well as achievement, and make fair decisions. The admissions process should also be a serious one for the student – requiring commitment from them, and real investment in the decision to enter higher education.

6.16 In addition, the Specialist Educational Needs and Disability Act, 2001 came into force from September 2002. It is now unlawful for the first time for institutions to discriminate against disabled students in how they admit students and in the services they provide for them.

6.17 UUK published a report earlier this month ("Fair Enough") which explores how universities can best ensure that they choose the most talented applicants, using a wide range of information and looking beyond raw qualifications. It looks at the way in which different institutions, well-aware that this is a critical but challenging issue, are taking a range of different steps to ensure that their admissions processes are fair.

6.18 Work is underway by the Qualifications and Curriculum Authority as part of its e-VIVA programme, due to be completed in July 2003, to pilot electronic records – 'e-portfolios' – which would offer university admissions offices a comprehensive picture of the abilities and experience of school leavers. The University of Bristol has developed a scheme which takes account of the results achieved by an applicant's school or college in making offers. Other top universities also apply flexible systems to identify those best able to take advantage of their courses. In the US, a number of leading universities operate schemes in which a proportion of their students, who might not otherwise qualify for admission, are admitted on the basis that they are in the top few per cent in their class. In Texas, there is evidence that such students catch up with those with higher entry scores by the time they graduate. In Leeds (see Box N below), the university offers additional support – financial, academic and pastoral – to students from non-traditional backgrounds, from before they apply to the university. In Durham, particular effort has been invested in converting applications into acceptances. And in Oxford and Cambridge, the difficulties inherent in running a collegiate admissions system in a sufficiently robust, rigorous and professional way to ensure that it is fair have been recognised. We welcome reforms being made by Oxford and Cambridge Universities to co-ordinate and centralise admissions, as part of ongoing efforts to widen access, and we would support their rapid extension.

BOX N: ROBERT OGDEN SCHOLARSHIPS AT THE UNIVERSITY OF LEEDS

Established in 1999, the Ogden scholarship scheme is aimed at widening participation amongst students from low participation neighbourhoods in Barnsley, Doncaster and Rotherham. Through both financial aid and student support the scheme helps students to remain in full time education beyond the age of 16 and, where appropriate, to progress to university. Financially, students from low-income families receive £500 in the first year of further education study and £1,000 in the second. Students who progress to the University of Leeds receive £2,000 in each year of study. Student support and guidance is provided through student mentoring and workshops that run prior to university applications. Subsequently, upon application, relevant Admission Tutors are informed of a student's scholar status and personal circumstances. Through these initiatives the scholarship scheme has enjoyed significant success. In 2001 there were 95 Ogden scholars, 72 of whom were engaged in post-16 education and 23 in undergraduate courses. 26 scholars were expected to register as undergraduates at the beginning of the 2002–03 academic year.

6.19 We welcome the work that has been done in individual institutions and by Universities UK, but believe that more can be done to ensure that across the sector best practice in admissions is shared and followed.

6.20 We intend to ask HEFCE, working with UUK, SCOP and UCAS to examine this issue in detail, and to consider ways in which best practice might be translated into a flexible framework for admissions processes which would help to ensure fairness and consistency. Once a framework is in place, it might form a pillar of the Access Agreements discussed below.

6.21 The sector should also consider the question of post-qualification applications, as suggested by the Tomlinson report into A-level standards. The Department for Education and Skills will work with higher education institutions, colleges, schools and awarding bodies to explore the way forward.

Setting Clear Benchmarks

6.22 If institutions and students are to be able to see clearly how well they are doing at improving fair access, good information needs to be available. Performance indicators published by the Funding Council give information on how well each institution recruits low participation groups and how that compares to 'benchmarks' based on what would be expected for an institution in similar circumstances, taking the qualifications and background of applicants into account. HEFCE have set improvement targets for year-on-year progress, initially up to 2004 and then to be revised up to 2010. HEFCE and UCAS are also looking to see whether data can be extracted to test whether there are any discrepancies in universities' admissions in respect of ethnicity.

6.23 The current ways of measuring access relate to social class, postcode and state/private school. The Government favours moving towards more sensitive indicators, looking at a student's family income, their parents' levels of education, and the average results of the school or college they attended. Data on family income could become available as early as 2004, and on school performance by 2006. We expect all of the new indicators to be in place by 2007 at the latest. We shall keep the existing criteria in place until we are satisfied with the robustness of the new data.

Targeted Funding

6.24 There is a cost to reaching out to students from less traditional backgrounds and offering them additional support once they are studying to make sure they fulfil their potential. The widening participation allocation, commonly known as the postcode premium, is intended to compensate institutions for these extra costs. But postcode analysis is a crude measure of disadvantage. Pockets of deprivation are often overlooked in affluent areas; and, conversely, many students who are not from disadvantaged backgrounds attract the premium. In consultation with HEFCE, we favour a reform of the premium to reflect the new access indicators of family income, parental levels of education, and the average results of the school attended, so that it better reflects need.

6.25 In addition, from 2003–04, the level of the premium will increase from around 5 per cent additional funding for each student from a disadvantaged background to around 20 per cent. This reflects a range of work that has been done, including a July 2002 study by the Education Select Committee which demonstrates that the cost of retaining non-traditional students is higher than had previously been estimated.

Bearing down on Drop-Out Rates

6.26 We also want to be sure that the premium is used properly to support these students through to successful completion of their degree – it must not be an incentive for recruiting students for whom higher education, or a particular course, is not suitable. Our low drop-out rates are a matter of national pride, but there is wide variation between institutions, with some approaching levels as unacceptably high as 40 per cent.

6.27 We know that the issue of drop-out is a complex one, and that flexible modes of learning, including credit transfer – as described in Chapter 5 – will do a great deal to help those students who wish to take a break from learning and then return, without the stigma of having 'dropped out', and without having to start again from scratch.

6.28 But we must make sure that institutions are not exploiting their most vulnerable students by making up the numbers with students who cannot cope; and we must also make sure that institutions support those who do have the potential for higher education, but need extra help to realise it. We will ask the Access Regulator to look into this question, and to develop a system of drop-out benchmarks which take into account the composition of the student body. The Regulator will have the power to fine those institutions that persistently fail to meet their benchmarks, and will be responsible for working with them to improve the position in other ways.

The Access Regulator

6.29 Those institutions that wish to charge variable fees will be required to have Access Agreements in place which set out the action they will take in order to safeguard and promote access, and the targets they will set for themselves. These will be determined by an independent Access Regulator, working with HEFCE and making use of their information and systems. The Regulator will ensure that the Agreements are robust and challenging. They will be monitored, and the Regulator will have the power to withdraw approval for variable fees, or impose financial penalties, if the Agreements are not fulfilled.

6.30 The Regulator would seek to extend current good practice through:

- More rigorous admissions regimes, based on the new admissions framework discussed above.

- Bursary schemes, and other financial measures.

- Proactive engagement with schools and colleges.

6.31 Institutions that do not wish to charge variable fees will be encouraged to use the services of the Regulator in establishing Access Agreements of their own, in order to quality assure their processes and give a guarantee to their students that they are fair and reliable.

Resources to support our strategy (£m)

	02–03	03–04	04–05	05–06	per cent Increase in cash terms in 05–06 over 02–03
AimHigher	39	69	81	83	113
Other initiatives	47	50	49	49	4
Total	86	119	130	132	53

Chapter 7
Freedoms and funding

Reform

The Government is making an unprecedented investment in the universities and will stand by them in future spending reviews. But to be really successful, universities must be free to take responsibility for their own strategic and financial future. Strong leadership and management, freed from excessive red tape, will help them not just to respond to change, but to drive it. And more financial freedom will allow them to fund their plans, and unleash their power to drive world-class research, innovative knowledge transfer, excellent teaching, high-quality, greater and more flexible provision, and fair access.

Key points and proposals

- Because leadership and management are key to the challenges ahead, we will help to fund HEFCE's and Universities UK's proposal for a new Leadership Foundation to support the sector to improve leadership and management.

- We will reduce bureaucracy and burdens on universities. A task force under David VandeLinde has been set up to report on further measures to reduce unnecessary red tape.

- Increasing university endowments is the route to real funding freedom in the long term. We will support institutions to build endowments in a range of ways.

- As we are asking new students to pay for the benefits they get from higher education, to build sustainable funding freedoms for the future, we believe that it is also right that those who have already benefited from higher education should be able to contribute.

- We will set up a task force to promote corporate as well as individual giving; and we propose to create a matched fund for endowment.

From 2006:

- We will give universities the freedom to set their own tuition fee, between £0 and £3,000. But no student or parent will have to pay any up-front fee. A new Graduate Contribution Scheme will allow them to pay their contribution back, through the tax system, once they are earning.

- We will safeguard access by having a maximum level for the graduate's contribution; by requiring institutions to develop strict Access Agreements; and by continuing to pay the first £1,100 of any contribution for those from lower-income backgrounds.

From 2005:

- We will raise the threshold at which loans start to be paid back from £10,000 to £15,000 a year, to make repayment less burdensome.

From 2004:

- We will increase the help available for the students that need it most, by introducing a new national grant of up to £1,000 a year for those from lower-income families. This will be in addition to the full existing student loan entitlement. We have already doubled the amount of extra money for vulnerable students and will introduce a new grant for part-time students.

- We are also simplifying and improving the administration of student support.

Introduction

7.1 The Government is overwhelmingly the biggest funder of higher education. Government funding will increase to around £10 billion a year by 2005–06 to support university students, teaching and research – a rise of over 6 per cent a year in real terms. This is equivalent to around £400 a year paid by every income tax payer in England, whether or not they personally gained from a university education. We believe that state support at this level is justified by the contribution of universities to the economy and society, and we will continue to stand by students and universities in future spending reviews. This Government will continue to increase its commitment to higher education.

7.2 However, in addition to this government support, higher education institutions need real freedom – including the freedom to raise their own funding, independent of government – if they are to flourish. They are already free and autonomous institutions, with the power to determine their academic and operational future; lead, manage, and appoint their own staff; determine their estates strategies; and manage their resources as they see fit. They may charge overseas students, part-time students, and post graduate students market rates for fees. But they do not always use the freedoms they have to the full; and as well as giving the sector new freedoms – as set out in this chapter – we want to empower them to use the ones they already have to their fullest potential, so that they can be dynamic and self-determining institutions.

Management and leadership

7.3   As the sector develops more freedom and self-determination, excellent leadership and management will become increasingly important. Universities are multi-million pound organisations with a vast array of different functions and components. They must split their resources between providing the capital infrastructure for both teaching and research, compete for the best staff, and often act as both landlord and major social centre for a large body of students. They have a key role within their communities and in their contribution to community leadership. In such a complicated environment, management poses exceptional challenges and, given the return to the economy, it is only right that the Government should seek to provide help where it can. Universities need the full range of professional skills among their managers and administrators.

LEADERSHIP FOUNDATION

7.4   Universities UK and HEFCE have proposed the creation of a Leadership Foundation to identify and meet key leadership and management needs across the sector, and build a cadre of professional leaders and managers. The Foundation will draw on the best international expertise in leadership and management, and will be associated with a prestigious higher education institution. It will also be charged with developing models of good practice in leadership and management. Once it is in place, the Leadership Foundation will take forward the key recommendations of the Lambert Review, announced by the Chancellor in November 2002, on how leadership and management can best support links between higher education and business. It will also work in partnership with the new Learning and Skills Leadership College.

RESEARCH FUNDING

7.5   In addition, measures on good governance and management will be linked with the new process for assessing larger research units (institutions or consortia), and rewarding them with extra funding, as set out in Chapter 2.

FREEING UP UNIVERSITIES FROM BUREAUCRACY

7.6   University managers tell us that unnecessary bureaucracy gets in the way of effective management. The sector itself has, with our endorsement, replaced a burdensome teaching quality assessment regime with a much lighter-touch process based on internal audit. But there is more that can be done.

7.7 The Better Regulation Task Force reported on bureaucracy in higher education this summer, and our response will say that we will:

- Ask HEFCE to test new proposals against the principles of good regulation;

- Consolidate funding into a smaller number of funding streams;

- Consider the reduction of unnecessarily burdensome audit;

- Reduce the burden of data collection.

7.8 In addition, we are working with HEFCE to reduce bureaucracy in a number of ways, which include:

- Working with other government bodies (like the TTA) to streamline their approaches to and demands on HEIs;

- Under the chairmanship of Sir Gareth Roberts, looking at the workings of research assessment.

7.9 To push the agenda forward further and faster, we have appointed David VandeLinde, Vice-Chancellor of Warwick University, to chair a taskforce to take a hard look at bureaucracy across the sector, building on the work of the Better Regulation Task Force and going beyond it to cut back bureaucracy wherever possible.

7.10 We have also considered whether the current structure of university regulation through the Privy Council represents an unnecessary burden. At present it is responsible for controlling degree-awarding powers, conferring 'University' title, and approving amendments to universities' statutes. It is essential to retain external control over both degree-awarding powers and university title, because the Government has a responsibility to make sure that standards are met before degrees can be awarded or an institution can become a university. Chapter 4 sets out the changes we propose in these areas. However, the Privy Council's powers to approve changes to the statutes of universities can delay institutional changes. Provided the important Nolan and Dearing reforms are safeguarded, we do not believe that the Privy Council needs to approve minor changes in the way universities go about their business. We will bring forward proposals with the Privy Council to lift this burden.

7.11 We know that there are regulatory issues arising from a number of the proposals in this document, and we intend to publish a regulatory impact assessment later in the year.

Structural change and development

7.12 Greater freedom and competition will compel institutions to improve their efficiency and management. Although there is some excellent leadership and management in the sector, some weaker institutions have been propped up rather than turned round. This is not in the interests of the student or the sector as a whole. There is still more scope to rationalise resources to improve cost effectiveness. Institutions are increasingly entering into strategic alliances and pooling their facilities. The sector is already starting to view institutional mergers, like the proposed merger between Manchester University and UMIST, as a path to success rather than as a response to failure. Mergers can considerably enhance an institution's standing in the academic community and increase its capacity to generate revenue from a number of sources.

7.13 Structural change can be a formidable undertaking. We are creating a strategic development fund, administered by HEFCE, to support change. The fund will support structural change including strategic alliances, merger and collaboration between higher education institutions, and between higher education and further education. It will also offer incentives for institutions to develop innovative programmes of study departing from the traditional 3 year full time model.

Funding

7.14 Chapter 1 sets out our generous settlement for higher education, which provides funding for the sector rising to almost £10 billion in 2005–06. This settlement goes a long way to putting right the backlog of underfunding of previous years, and, more importantly, to beginning the process of reform which will lay the foundations for the future. However, funding for higher education has to be made sustainable for the long term, not just the life of this spending review, and we need a system that enables universities to build up both their funding and their independence. Universities need to compete in the world market, and leading universities in other countries will be able to draw on extensive private funding.

7.15 There is a general recognition among our universities that although they look to the Government to fund teaching and research, it is unrealistic to expect the Government to match the total funding levels of the world's best-endowed universities. It follows that giving greater financial freedom to our universities will mean increasing the financial underpinning of the sector; widening the number and type of sources of finance available to it; and reducing dependence on government.

Independence through Endowment

7.16 The way forward is through endowment. This will ensure the sector is less dependent on any single source of funding, as well as enabling it to take advantage of new opportunities that they could not otherwise afford. Endowment funds can be used, for example, to make financial investments; invest in new facilities, enabling universities to bid for research funds where the infrastructure costs are not covered; pay for specific chairs or general academic posts; undertake research, and pay researchers competitively and create scholarship funds. Harvard spends at least $100 million a year from its endowment fund to support its student financial aid scheme. British universities have much smaller endowments than their global competitors. Harvard has about $18 billion, Yale $11 billion and Princeton $8 billion. In contrast, Oxford has about £2 billion.[42]

7.17 We need to ensure that we have a culture in which donors and all our institutions, including those with no history of incentivising donations, make the most of the potential of endowment. We want to build the culture of giving as much as possible, both from individuals and from business. We have developed a range of measures to build the giving culture:

- **Giving something back:** We now ask students going through higher education to contribute something to its cost. But there are many who had their higher education free, and have reaped enormous individual benefits from it. If we are to support the sector, we believe that it is right to ask them to contribute too. It will be made possible, as for other charities, for taxpayers, through Gift Aid and through the income tax form directly, to contribute tax repayments voluntarily to higher education institutions. Those who feel that they cannot afford to do this, or who do not wish to do so, need not contribute; but we believe that it is only right that if future graduates are to contribute, those who have already benefited should be encouraged to do so.

- **Promoting individual giving:** We will also promote individual giving by making the benefits clearer. Because universities are charities, individuals can use Gift Aid if they are taxpayers, and higher rate taxpayers can claim back the higher rate element of tax on the value of donation. Alumni and others need to understand better not only what the benefits are to them but also benefits and advantages that charitable status brings to universities. We expect the task force we are setting up (below) to address this as part of its promotion campaign, including how we can make this clearer through the tax system.

- We will also encourage the sector to develop a **standard gift aid form** for giving – as individual donors and their advisers have said that such a form would help.

- **Promoting corporate giving.** There are already generous tax incentives for companies to make donations to universities or their charitable offshoots. Companies can claim full tax relief for any donations they make provided they use the Gift Aid mechanism; they can also

---

42 As of end July 2002, including combined endowments and other reserves of all colleges (estimated at £1.6 billion), as well as the university's overall endowment (£390 million).

claim full tax relief for money provided as sponsorship if there is some business benefit. We will set up a **task force** to encourage institutions and potential donors to promote the existing incentives for individual and corporate donation and to encourage change in university and individual behaviour. The task force would be composed of corporate donors, financial and fundraising experts, from the public, private and voluntary sectors, and the HE sector itself, as well as other key opinion formers. It would also look at other entrepreneurial activity and how that could be developed.

7.18 To provide direct assistance to the sector:

■ We will seek the resources for a time limited, matched endowment fund to which any university can apply. We want to explore how we could provide matched funding which would incentivise university fund-raising from individuals, companies and other sources such as the disposal of under-used assets. The allocation mechanism would take account of universities' existing fund-raising capacity. We shall publish criteria, which are likely to include capital renewal, research, and bursaries for poorer students. We are exploring potential sources of funding. If alternative sources are not available, we would consider funding from existing Departmental budgets.

■ The professionalisation of fundraising activities can also be a driver for good financial management. Donors want tangible evidence of how their money has been used, and what could not be done without it. In order to gain funds the organisation has to be demonstrably excellent both in its fundraising and in its management of those given funds.

The contribution from graduates

7.19 Endowment funds have the potential to provide universities with increased resources and freedoms. But inevitably it will take a long time for endowments to build up to levels which make a significant contribution to revenue. In the short term the government is putting in very significant extra funding to reverse the decline in our universities but there are, of course, competing pressures on public spending – not least provision for early years, schools and post-16 learning. So although the government will continue to remain the major funder of universities and we will work with universities to develop endowments, we also need to look to other sources of income – in addition to those from government – to sustain a strong and thriving higher education sector.

7.20 The principle that it is right for students to make a contribution to the costs of their course was established by Lord Dearing in 1997. It is now generally accepted, and raises £450 million a year. But universities have asked us to consider whether students might be asked to contribute more to the cost of their education.

7.21 Currently students who pay the full £1,100 fee are only contributing about a quarter of the average cost of their university teaching and education – the taxpayer still pays the rest. Our student support package is one of the most generous in the world. Graduates derive substantial benefits from having gained a degree, including wider career opportunities and the financial benefits that generally follow. On average those with a higher education qualification earn around 50% more than non-graduates.

7.22 Given these benefits to an individual from the investment in a university education, the government has decided that it is fair to allow universities, if they so determine, to ask students to make an increased contribution – as they do in Australia, New Zealand, Canada and the United States. We believe that this will also have the benefit of enhancing the independence of universities by making them less reliant on government funding.

7.23 But if universities are to be given the freedom to raise higher contributions from students, they must be able to demonstrate that they will safeguard access, and so no university will be allowed to raise its fees until it has an Access Agreement in place (see Chapter 6). In addition:

- The level of contributions must be low enough to be manageable, and costs should still be shared with the taxpayer;

- Payments should only be made by those who can afford them – this will mean allowing graduates to pay contributions once they are earning, rather than being asked to pay any fee up-front.

It will also be important for universities to have the governance, leadership and management arrangements in place to ensure that fee income delivers overall value for money in improving the quality of teaching and learning facilities for students.

Different fees for different courses

7.24 We have carefully considered the question of whether an additional contribution should be paid at a flat rate – so that it is the same wherever and whatever a student studies – or whether it should vary according to institution and course.

7.25 It is absolutely clear that students get different returns from different courses. The graph below shows the different earnings premia obtained by women students taking different degree subjects.[43]

43 The return to education: evidence from the Labour Force Survey, Walker and Zhu, 2001. The percentages shown are in terms of hourly earnings.

Figure 4: Earnings premia of degree subjects for women, 1993–1999

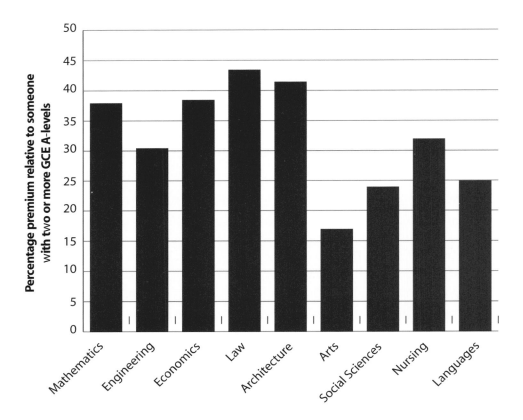

7.26 More recent research found a 44 percentage point difference in average returns between graduates from institutions at the two extremes of the graduate pay scale.[44]

7.27 We believe that a revised contribution system should recognise these differences properly, and not ask students who can't expect such good prospects in the labour market to subsidise those that can, through a flat fee.

7.28 This also means that institutions will be able to reap rewards for offering courses that serve students well. It will make student choice a much more powerful force, and help choice drive quality.

7.29 We do recognise, though, that a wholly unregulated variable fee scheme could pose dangers to access, with universities setting fee levels that some students simply could not afford. Our challenge has been to combine the benefits of variable contributions while making certain that fair access is not threatened.

44 Financial Returns to undergraduates and tuition fees, Dr Gavan Conlon and Arnaud Chevalier, November 2002, CIHE.

The Graduate Contribution Scheme

7.30 On the basis of these key principles, from the academic year 2006/07 we have decided to abolish up-front tuition fees, and allow universities to set their own rates for graduate contributions, between £0 and £3,000 a year. These contributions can be paid back once a graduate is earning, through a new Graduate Contribution Scheme, which will link monthly repayments to earnings through the tax system. Robust safeguards will protect access for all students. These are described below.

Safeguards for students

CAP ON FEES

7.31 The maximum total contribution a university will be able to set will be £3,000 per year from Autumn 2006. There will be no minimum fee – so for some courses, fees might go down. This cap will apply throughout the life of the next Parliament, and it will rise annually in line with inflation so that it keeps its real value.

AGREEMENT ON ACCESS

7.32 Universities will, as described in Chapter 6, have to have Access Agreements approved by the independent Access Regulator before they are allowed to introduce a contribution higher than the current standard fee. The Access Agreement will commit universities to take action to increase the take up of university places from the most disadvantaged groups. The regulator will have the power to withdraw their right to vary the graduate contribution, or impose financial penalties, if the university does not fulfil its Agreement. The Government believes that this is a particularly powerful incentive for increasing the proportion of those from the most disadvantaged groups attending our leading universities, and is confident that most of these universities will welcome this measure.

HELP WITH CONTRIBUTIONS FOR THOSE THAT NEED IT MOST

7.33 Under the current system the Government spends over £400 million on paying the fees of those whose parents are least able to afford the standard £1,100 fee. This sum pays the fee in full for those whose parents are on incomes up to £20,000. For those between £20,000 and £30,000, it covers part of the cost of the fee. The Government will continue this spending on student support when the new contribution arrangements come into effect in 2006. This will reduce any contribution that students have to pay by up to £1,100 (at current prices – by 2006 the level will be higher, because the current standard fee rises each year to keep pace with inflation).

7.34 This means that students currently having their full fee paid by the Government will, under the new system, not have to pay any contribution if they study on a course where the university does not choose to put up the rate. If the university asks for a higher contribution, such a student will only pay the difference between the higher fee and the Government's support – at current prices, that would mean that instead of paying £3,000 for a top-priced course, they would only have to pay £1,900.

7.35 In order to make sure that the help really reaches those that need it most, we are updating the parental income assessment so that it is fairer and recognises changes in family patterns. Currently the income of a step-parent is not counted in the means-test for fees and loans. For fairness and consistency, we will adopt the more inclusive definition of household income used by the Inland Revenue.

GRANTS

7.36 We have listened to those who say that those from the poorest backgrounds need additional incentives and financial help to continue in full-time education. So, those students with parents on the lowest incomes starting full-time higher education courses will be eligible for a new Higher Education Grant of up to £1,000 a year. We will start this grant as soon as we can – from Autumn 2004. Students from households with incomes of £10,000 or less will receive the full award and some grant will be available to those whose families earn up to £20,000 a year. This grant will absorb the current Opportunity Bursaries, an important but smaller-scale programme that operates only in certain areas.

7.37 A student coming from a family earning less than £10,000 a year will therefore be entitled to £1,100 in fee support, and £1,000 in grant, as well as the full student loan for living costs – currently £3,905 for students studying away from home, and more in London – meaning that they have almost £5,000 a year to live on, as well as help with their graduate contribution.

7.38 We will allocate almost £300m to support these arrangements. For the period after 2006, we will continue with this level of resource, but will carefully review these arrangements to see whether they best assist access for those from the poorest groups, and properly serve the needs of the most vulnerable students. We will consider whether we could target these resources better, for example in remitting graduate fee contributions above the £1,100 level, perhaps by building schemes that work in partnership with universities' own bursary schemes.

RIGHT TO DEFER FEES, AND PAY AT A RATE THAT DEPENDS ON INCOME

7.39 No student will have to pay their contribution up-front or while they are studying, although they will, of course, be able to do so if they wish. Every student, irrespective of their own means or those of their parents, will be able to pay their Graduate Contribution after they leave university, and are earning. This means that higher education will continue to be open to everyone with the potential to benefit and no-one will have to contribute to the cost of their course until they can afford to do so.

7.40 Those students who defer payment through the Graduate Contribution Scheme will have the cost collected after graduation once they are in employment. Students will be able to defer their fees on the same basis as for the current student maintenance loans. This means that the amount deferred will be uprated for inflation. They will, as with the current system for repaying maintenance loans, make payments through the tax system at the rate of 9 per cent of their income above a certain threshold, so that graduates repay at a rate they can afford.

7.41 To make payments less burdensome for every graduate, we shall raise the repayment threshold at which payments start being made, from £10,000 to £15,000 a year. This increased threshold will apply to student loans for living costs too, and will apply from 2005. The change will mean a reduction in repayments of £450 a year for every graduate earning £15,000 or more (those earning less than £15,000 would not have to start to repay at all). This means that the payments will be more manageable, particularly for those on lower incomes, but repayment may be phased over a longer period.

7.42 Students will be able to make additional payments at any time to reduce the amount owed. (They might do so through higher monthly payments, gifts from parents and family, the proceeds of work through university or employers' recruitment incentive payments.)

7.43 Students paying larger contributions will expect to see the income generated going into improved teaching and facilities. Universities will only be able to do this if they have available to them the extra cash from the contributions they set. The Government will, therefore, provide income to universities equal to the contribution levels they have set. The Government will then receive the payment back from students over time.

Improved Support for Part-Time Students

7.44 We propose to improve the package of support for part-time students dramatically, to make sure that we are properly supporting those who study more flexibly.

- There will be guaranteed fee support (up to an annual capped maximum) applied for through LEAs for those whose income is below certain thresholds and who are studying courses that are at least half-time.

- We will introduce a new grant of £250 to meet the cost of books, travel and other course expenditure which will be available to all those entitled to fee support. This will replace an existing loan.

- Specific funding will be identified for the first time within the Access to Learning Fund to provide childcare grants for those who are getting statutory fee support and are on courses that are at least half-time.

- Institutions will also be able to use the Access to Learning Fund to provide discretionary fee waivers and help towards the other costs of study for certain part-time students on a low income studying the equivalent of at least 12 credits (10% of a full-time course).

Independence at 18

7.45 These reforms take an important step in the direction of treating students as independent adults at 18. The Graduate Contribution Scheme means that no student need rely on their parents to pay for the cost of their tuition, and in the context of the next comprehensive spending review, we will consider other changes to parental means-testing.

The Public Sector Workforce

7.46 All employers of graduates have an interest in ensuring that there are enough new graduates with the right skills to meet their needs. This applies as much to the public as the private sector; the role of higher education in training key public sector workers is vital. We believe that, overall, our proposed reforms – including in particular the expansion of foundation degrees focused on the needs of the public as well as the private sectors – will help public sector recruitment by increasing the pool of qualified graduates.

7.47 One of our main concerns in developing the new arrangements will be to make sure that they do not discourage our brightest young people from all backgrounds entering training for, or taking jobs in, the public sector. Over time, different public services have responded to changing labour market pressures in different ways. For very many public sector graduates, the gain from a university education will be more than they are asked to pay back. Some public sector employers already help meet the costs of higher education for certain key staff, through different mechanisms which fit their particular needs. Box O gives some examples. Individual departments and employers will, as now, need to look at the impact of these proposals on their labour markets and decide, in the light of available resources, what steps to take to support public service modernisation and recruitment and retention.

7.48 This means that approaches will be part of carefully costed and planned programmes to modernise and develop the public sector workforce, and to recruit and retain staff in a targeted way. Across government, we will explore the best ways of doing this effectively, taking account of the different situations in each sector. Any such measures will need to be funded from within the departmental spending plans then in force.

BOX O: CURRENT ARRANGEMENTS FOR THE PUBLIC SECTOR WORKFORCE

Teachers – PGCE courses are already exempted from the standard tuition fee, and more incentives are currently being introduced, by writing off teachers' student loans (which started in September 2002), usually over ten years, provided they continue to teach a shortage subject and remain in teaching for a certain period.

Doctors and dentists – At present, the Department of Health meets the costs of fees for medical and dental students in the fifth or later years of their courses.

Nurses, midwives, and allied health professions – The NHS contracts directly with HEIs for the provision of training to nurses, midwives, and allied health professions, who pay no tuition fees.

Social work – From September 2003, students studying social work will have their fee contributions met by the Department of Health.

7.49 Of course, similar issues arise for other employers, in professions like law and architecture, and in science and engineering. We expect that these employers too will consider schemes to make sure that they can bring through the graduates they need.

CROSS-BORDER ISSUES

7.50 The package of student funding to which students are entitled depends on which UK country they ordinarily live in. So students from Scotland will continue to be entitled to the package of loans and grants made available through the Student Awards Agency for Scotland, and students from Northern Ireland will continue to be entitled to the package of loans and grants made available through the Northern Ireland Education and Library Boards. In Wales, although institutional funding for higher education is devolved, funding for student support is not.

7.51 Because repayments are made through the tax system, and at present each of the devolved nations uses the same system for repaying fees (or, in Scotland, the Graduate Endowment), the increase in the repayment threshold from £10,000 to £15,000 will apply across the UK.

7.52 We will need to consider further the impact of our proposals for student and institutional funding on flows of students between UK countries. We will discuss these issues with the devolved administrations.

EUROPEAN STUDENTS

7.53 The UK has an excellent reputation in Europe for delivering high quality courses in higher education, and significant numbers of EU nationals undertake higher education in the UK. The reciprocal arrangements with Europe mean that EU students should be supported on the same basis as home students for the costs of their tuition, but not for the costs of their maintenance. So European students who take higher education courses in England will, like the UK students, be required to pay fees of up to £3,000.

EXTENDING SUPPORT AND SIMPLIFYING THE SYSTEM

7.54 The Government is making a number of other changes to the student support system to bring it up to date with a more diverse student population, and to help to promote wider access.

- We will be carrying out a survey into the levels of maintenance support needed for basic living costs – the next Student Income and Expenditure Survey – and will review our arrangements carefully in the light of the results.

- We have doubled the support available for the most vulnerable.

- We are creating a much more generous package for part-time students, including a new books and equipment grant to replace the current loan.

- We have simplified the number of funding streams.

- We will make the process of applying for support simpler.

- We will reflect the non-commercial nature of the loan, by preventing student loans forming part of a bankrupt's estate.

Annex C gives more details of these changes.

Improving Awareness

7.55 No system of student support will be effective unless it is understood. From 2003–04 onwards, we will be increasing the amount of student support explanation and promotion to prospective students, their families and advisors. We will increase the awareness of potential students of the amount of support available to them in higher education and we will target our efforts at traditionally under-represented groups in higher education. This will form part of the Department's existing AimHigher campaign.

Conclusion

1   Our universities are central to the health of our economy and of our democracy. They want – and we want them – to be among the best in the world. If we are to continue to achieve that aim and to move towards the vision set out in Chapter 1 of this strategy, then the challenges we face are:

- To recognise and encourage diversity of role, with universities and colleges proud to be different and to play to their individual strengths.

- To develop the way we use public funding so as to stimulate greater success and higher quality in teaching, research, knowledge transfer, widening participation and economic and cultural impact on the community.

- For all universities and colleges to be committed to fair access for students from all backgrounds, to serving the whole community and to increasing the economic health of their region and the country as a whole.

- To improve the economic contribution that universities and colleges make through innovation, improving the skills of the nation and stimulating new businesses in a increasingly competitive world.

- To welcome changes in the shape and structure of the sector which will bring new forms of collaboration between higher education institutions, and between them and FE colleges.

- To invest in even more effective leadership and management, so as to be able to meet the tasks ahead and to take advantage of the greater freedom which will flow from new funding sources.

- And for universities and colleges to continue to embody the values which are central to a democratic society.

2   Our proposals are designed to meet those challenges. We shall welcome comments on them and will consult further as we implement our strategy in partnership with all of those involved.

What happens next?

1   Following the launch of the strategy document there will be:

- A period for comment, until 30 April 2003

- Early legislation to underpin the proposals

- Implementation of the strategy, beginning in September 2003

Your opportunity to tell us what you think

2   After the launch of the document there will be a period for comment, in which the Government will be engaging in a wide-ranging dialogue with those who provide higher education and those who benefit from it.

3   The period for comment will run until 30 April 2003.

If you would like to send comments:

Written responses should be sent to:
Consultation Unit
Department for Education & Skills
Area 1D
Castle View House
East Lane
Runcorn
Cheshire WA7 2GJ

You can also respond by e-mail to:

hestrategy@dfes.gsi.gov.uk

4   Please ensure the comments reach us by 30 April 2003. A summary of the comments will be available on the higher education website shortly after the end of the period (www.dfes.gov.uk/highereducation/hestrategy).

Confidentiality

5   All replies will be considered, providing they reach us by the deadline. We may want to use your comments publicly and to attribute them to you or the organisation you represent.

6   If you would prefer your comments to be kept confidential, please make that clear in your response.

Contact point

7   If you have further questions about the consultation please contact the DfES Consultation Unit on 01928 794888.

Workshops

8   During the period for comment, we will hold regional workshops involving universities and colleges, key partners such as HEFCE, the LSC and the Teacher Training Agency, and other bodies such as Universities UK, the Standing Conference of Principals and the NUS. We shall also invite a wide range of other key partners, such as Connexions personal advisers.

Young People and their Families

9   We have published alongside the strategy document an information leaflet, intended primarily for students, potential students and their families, which summarises the main proposals. We are sending the leaflet to schools with sixth forms and making it available in other ways, for example through student unions and the Connexions Service.

10   We want to reach as many young people as possible. We will make copies of both documents available to schools and colleges, as well as placing the full document and the information leaflet for young people on the Young People's Website (www.dfes.gov.uk/youngpeople),

11   We want parents to join in the debate too and are encouraging this by using the Parents' Website (www.dfes.gov.uk/parents), where parents will find the full document and the summary version.

Legislation

12   In 2003–04 the Government will be introducing legislation to underpin the proposals in the Strategy Document.

Implementing the Strategy

13   Annex A outlines the phases of delivery for our Strategy.

Annex A

Higher education strategy: Phases of delivery

Phase One: Short term (2003-2005)

- Criteria in place for a higher research category

- From 2004/05, £500 million per year for science research infrastructure

- 2004/05 Arts and Humanities Research Council in operation

- Promising Researcher Fellowship scheme begins

- First Knowledge Exchanges identified

- RDAs increasingly involved in distribution of HEIF

- First Centres of Excellence in Teaching identified

- Professional standards for teaching established

- Easy-to-Use Guide to Universities published

- Teaching Quality Academy established

- Changes to University title to make it dependent on teaching

- Improved training and induction arrangements in place for external examiners

- Statutory adjudicator for student complaints in place

- Further work on credit transfer scheme carried out

- Integration of HNDs and HNCs into foundation degree framework

- Access premium and benchmarks reformed with income and school type measures in place

- AimHigher brought together with Partnerships for Progression and Excellence Challenge

- Admissions Review completed

- Independent Access Regulator set up following legislation

- Grants introduced for new students

- Income threshold at which repayments are made rises to £15,000

- Changed role of Privy Council in approving changes to university statutes

- Leadership Foundation established

- Lambert and Innovation Reviews report

Phase Two: Medium term (2005-2007)

- Expenditure on science and research increases by £1.25 billion compared to 2002–03

- HEIF rises to £90m by 2005–06

- More Knowledge Exchanges identified

- All new teachers receive accredited training

- More Centres of Excellence in teaching identified

- Independent Access Regulator ensures access agreements are in place before allowing universities to charge fees

- Universities introduce Graduate Contribution Scheme in 2006/07

Phase Three: Longer term (2007 and beyond)

- Implementation of the revised RAE

- Increased collaboration between research departments and institutions

- Quality incentives for teaching in the pay system

- Foundation degree growth sustained

- Access firmly secured for all

- Arrangements for universities introducing Graduate Contribution Scheme embedded

- First repayments of student loans under the Graduate Contribution Scheme

Annex B
Work to reduce bureaucracy in higher education

There is clearly a balance to be struck in order to preserve accountability while removing burdens, but this Government already takes the issue of unnecessary bureaucracy very seriously, and action is under way to cut burdens in higher education. For example:

- The new quality assurance process for universities, replacing the often burdensome TQA, is a single process instead of two, and is much lighter-touch, relying more heavily on institutions' own internal audit processes; time-consuming subject inspection will only be necessary where there are concerns about performance.

- Sir Gareth Roberts is leading a review of research assessment reporting to the UK funding bodies. The review is focusing on improving the process of research assessment, including eliminating unnecessary bureaucracy.

- HEFCE bidding processes have been redesigned using two stage processes allowing institutions to spend less time on bids that do not have a realistic chance of success.

- Some funding streams (e.g. for capital and rewarding and developing staff) from HEFCE are now handled on a 'conditional allocations' basis cutting down on the need for institutions to bid.

- HEFCE and the Office for Science and Technology (OST) both contributed to the Science Research Infrastructure Fund (SRIF) to produce one cross-departmental funding mechanism.

- HEFCE has reduced its institutional audit from 5 days every 3 years to a similar period every 5 years. It now spends more time with those institutions at greatest risk.

- Thresholds for audit certificates for capital projects were raised from £250k to £1m, reducing the need for (and cost) of external validation of claims.

- The NHS are redesigning their contracts with HEIs using benchmark processes and reducing the bureaucratic burden.

- HEFCE and the TTA have combined resources to deliver the rewarding and developing staff initiative.

- The QAA, Ofsted and ALI are working together to reduce inspection burdens in FE colleges, while preserving standards and accountability.

- Ministers have already agreed that the Higher Education Statistics Agency (HESA) December data return – which is a census survey of all students in UK higher education – need no longer be collected with effect from December 2002. This eliminates a large time-consuming exercise, at a time when institutions are also making returns to other bodies about students.

Annex C
Extending and simplifying student support

1   We are spending nearly a quarter of a billion pounds in 2002–03 on additional support for students with particular financial needs, compared to £124m five years ago. This is made up of a number of statutory grants for those with children or disabilities, as well as discretionary grants and loans for those in financial difficulty, and bursaries for some students from disadvantaged backgrounds. There are also fee waivers and loans for those studying part-time. This greatly increased provision has helped to encourage more non-traditional students into higher education, especially mature students with children. But the system has become over-complex and difficult for students to understand and access, and an administrative burden for some institutions.

2   A review of this targeted student support was carried out by the Department last year. The review group was led by Dr Philip Harris, of Manchester University, and included administrators and student advisers from a number of Universities, as well as LEAs, and the NUS. The outcome of the review provides a coherent, simplified and easier to understand package of support for full-time students with children. More support is now available up-front, giving students more certainty over what they will get before they start their courses. Funding for students who get into financial difficulties while studying will be simpler and entirely grant-based. By 2004/05 instead of 14 different funds for vulnerable students there will be 5. The review also proposed an improved package of support for part-time students, which we are implementing.

3   Alongside these simpler, improved financial arrangements, we are also making the administration simpler. Together with the Student Loans Company, the Department is taking forward a programme to modernise the delivery of student support. During 2003–04 there will be pilots of a new IT system and a streamlined application process. This will be extended across all LEAs in England from 2004–05, subject to successful piloting. By 2004 our intention is that most students will have to fill in fewer, shorter forms to get the support they need. They will also have a choice over how they get advice on the help available, and how they apply for it – over the internet as well as on paper.

4   We are updating the parental income assessment so that it is fairer and recognises changes in family patterns. Currently the income of a step-parent is not counted in the means-test for fees and loans. This is inconsistent with the more inclusive definition of household income used in the tax and benefits system and it means that families with a step-parent currently pay less than families with two natural parents, even if the two families' financial circumstances are the same. So, for fairness and consistency, we will adopt the definition of household income used by the Inland Revenue.

5   The detail of the changes is set out below:

SIMPLIFIED SUPPORT FOR THOSE WITH DEPENDANTS

- The system will be simplified so that most student parents will get help for their dependants through two grants. In addition, all student parents with household incomes below £58,000 will be eligible for support through tax credits, many for the first time. This will provide a seamless and easy transition for those parents going from benefits to university or work.

- Student parents will see no reduction in their support – some will be better-off, and they will have much greater certainty over their funding before they start their courses.

- From 2003–04, there will be a new Parents Learning Allowance of up to £1,300 to meet course related costs, replacing 3 existing grants.[45] Most student parents will get the full £1,300 grant.[46]

- The Childcare Grant will remain available for those using registered childcare and it will be increased to meet 85% of actual costs across the whole academic year.[47]

- The new Child Tax Credits and passported free school meals will replace School Meals Grant and Dependants Grant for students with children.

- The Adult Dependants Grant will continue to provide support for students who have other adults financially dependent on them.[48]

SIMPLER AND MORE TRANSPARENT ARRANGEMENTS FOR STUDENTS IN FINANCIAL DIFFICULTY

- We are merging hardship loans and funds for 2004–05 into a single one stop discretionary fund administered through universities and colleges – the Access to Learning Fund (AtLF).

- All payments from the Access to Learning Fund will be in the form of non-repayable grants.

- More detailed guidance will be provided for institutions to ensure that the Fund is operated on a consistent and transparent basis across all institutions.

45 The grants which are being replaced by the Parents Learning Allowance are the Additional Dependants Grant (£255), Travel, Books and Equipment Grant (£500) and Access Bursary (£500).

46 2003–04 rate.

47 Up to £5,967 for one child, or up to £ 8,840 for two or more children in 2003–04.

48 £2,280 in 2003–04, subject to income.

- A new method of allocating the Fund to institutions, taking account of students' financial circumstances and regional differences in living costs, will direct resources better to where they are most needed.

SUPPORT FOR DISABLED STUDENTS

- Disabled Student Allowances have already been extended to part-time and postgraduates and are no longer subject to means-test.

- These Allowances will continue as now but we are speeding up the application process.

- There will be more access centres for assessments and clearer guidance for administrators so that disabled students can apply for assessment of their needs much earlier and get their support in place before they start.

IMPROVED SUPPORT FOR PART-TIME STUDENTS

We propose to improve the package of support for part-time students dramatically, to make sure that we are properly supporting those who study more flexibly:

- There will be guaranteed fee support (up to an annual capped maximum) applied for through LEAs for those whose income is below certain thresholds, and who are studying courses that are at least half-time.

- We will introduce a new grant of £250 to meet the cost of books, travel and other course expenditure which will be available to all those entitled to fee support. This will replace an existing loan.

- Specific funding will be identified for the first time within the Access to Learning Fund to provide childcare grants for those who are getting statutory fee support, and are on courses that are at least half-time.

- Institutions will also be able to use the Access to Learning Fund to provide discretionary fee waivers and help towards the other costs of study for certain part-time students on a low income studying the equivalent of at least 12 credits (10% of a full-time course).

MODERNISING THE APPLICATION PROCESS

We are modernising and simplifying the processes by which students are paid support so that:

- students need to complete fewer application forms;

- the burden on students to provide information and evidence is reduced; and

- students can apply for and obtain information about the support available through new electronic channels and on the internet.

5 We do not want the financial support arrangements to act as a barrier to students. Students need to be clear about the amount of financial support available not only when they start their courses but also if they change course including switching between full- and part-time study. Policies also need to be flexible and forward looking enough to accommodate changing modes of study. Continuous review is the key to ensuring that future policy is developed so that those who need financial support have access to it.

Annex D
Glossary

AHRB – the Arts and Humanities Research Board. The body that allocates funding for specific research projects in the arts and humanities.

ALI – the Adult Learning Inspectorate

Brain-drain – The reported loss of academic talent in the UK to competition overseas

BRTF – The Better Regulation Task Force, a group that was set up to assess where bureaucracy could be cut.

FE – Further Education

FEC – Further Education College

Foundation degrees (FDs) – new two year qualifications with a focus on supplying the skills employers need.

HE – Higher Education

HEFCE – the Higher Education Funding Council for England

HEIs – Higher Education Institutions

HEIF – the Higher Education Innovation Fund. Provides funding to support 'knowledge transfer' activities.

HESDA – Higher Education Staff Development Agency

HND/HNC – Higher National Diplomas and Higher National Certificates. Forms of 'sub-degree' qualification in HE.

ICT – Information and Communications Technology

ILTHE – the Institute of Learning and Teaching in Higher Education

LSC – the Learning and Skills Council

LTSN – Learning and Teaching Support Network

OECD – the Organisation for Economic Co-operation and Development

QAA – the Quality Assurance Agency for Higher Education

RAE – the Research Assessment Exercise. Currently the process by which HEFCE allocates research funding.

RDAs – Regional Development Agencies

Research councils – The bodies that allocate research funding provided by the Office of Science and Technology (OST) to support specific research projects.

SCOP – the Standing Conference of Principals

Sector Skills Councils – bodies with responsibility for ensuring that the skills needs of their industry 'sector' are met.

Spending Review – The process that determines Government expenditure for the next three years. It replaces the annual Public Expenditure Survey.

Spin-out company – A business set up by staff at an HEI to make use of the commercial applications of research.

Transparency Review – A report on the distribution of expenditure on research and teaching in HEIs across the UK.

TTA – the Teacher Training Agency

UCAS – the Universities and Colleges Admissions Service

UUK – Universities UK

Printed in the UK for The Stationery Office Limited
on behalf of the Controller of Her Majesty's Stationery Office
ID 127837 1/03